PARIS *MADE EASY*

Andy in Paris

ABOUT THE AUTHOR
Andy Herbach is a lawyer and resides in Milwaukee. He is the co-author of the Eating & Drinking on the Open Road Series of menu readers and restaurant guides, including *Eating & Drinking in Paris, Eating & Drinking in Italy, Eating & Drinking in Spain* and *Eating & Drinking in Latin America*. He is also the author of *Provence Made Easy* (Spring 2005). You can e-mail him corrections, additions, and comments at eatndrink@aol.com or through his website at www.eatndrink.com.

PARIS MADE EASY

Andy Herbach
Co-author of *Eating & Drinking in Paris*

Open Road Publishing

Open Road Publishing

We offer travel guides to American and foreign locales. Our books tell it like it is, often with an opinionated edge, and our experienced authors always give you all the information you need to have the trip of a lifetime. Write for your free catalog of all our titles.

Open Road Publishing
P.O. Box 284, Cold Spring Harbor, NY 11724
E-mail: Jopenroad@aol.com

Acknowledgments

The Culinary Walk was written with Michael Dillon.
French editor: Marie Fossier
English editors: Jonathan Stein and Marian Olson
Website (www.eatndrink.com): McDill Design
and Susan Chwae
Additional research: Karl Raaum

TABLE OF CONTENTS

Introduction   7

1. Sights   8
    The Islands   8
    1st and 2nd Arrondissements   14
    3rd and 4th Arrondissements   23
    5th Arrondissement   32
    6th Arrondissement   39
    7th Arrondissement   45
    8th Arrondissement   53
    16th Arrondissement   62
    9th Arrondissement   66
    10th Arrondissement   70
    11th Arrondissement   72
    12th Arrondissement   74
    13th Arrondissement   75
    14th and 15th Arrondissements   77
    17th Arrondisement   81
    18th Arrondissement   82
    19th Arrondissement   88
    20th Arrondissement   89
    Off The Beaten Path   90
    Excursions   91

2. Walks   95
    Islands Walk   95
    Left Bank Walk   99
    Marais Walk   102
    Major Sights Walk   105
    Montmartre Walk   108
    Culinary Walks   111

3. Miscellany   113

Tips on Budget Dining   113
Paris by Month   113
The Bridges of Paris   115
Resources   116
  Hotel Sidebar   119
  Helpful Phrases Sidebar   123

Index   123

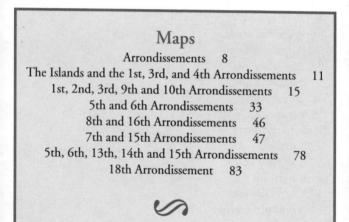

Maps

Arrondissements   8
The Islands and the 1st, 3rd, and 4th Arrondissements   11
1st, 2nd, 3rd, 9th and 10th Arrondissements   15
5th and 6th Arrondissements   33
8th and 16th Arrondissements   46
7th and 15th Arrondissements   47
5th, 6th, 13th, 14th and 15th Arrondissements   78
18th Arrondissement   83

INTRODUCTION

Paris is the most fabulous city in the world, not because of the Eiffel Tower or the Champs-Élysées, but because there's simply no other place in the world like it.

It's called the City of Light, but perhaps it should be called the City of Promise. Around every corner is the promise of another beautiful street, another bistro filled with people eating delicious food (Paris is a city where you have to work at having a bad meal), another building that in any other city would be remarkable, but in Paris is just another building. Walk down practically any block in Paris, and the sights, smells and sounds will excite you.

Sure, it's a city where people live and work, except in Paris, they carry *baguettes*, stop at sidewalk cafés, and have a leisurely cup of coffee or glass of wine (and yes, a cigarette or two). Paris is also a large metropolis, home to millions. It's incredibly diverse, and most Parisians embrace that diversity.

As our title says, this little guide—like Paris itself—will make you a promise too: we'll make your trip to Paris easy. Tuck our book into your pocket and you'll have the city at your fingertips, from the familiar Arc de Triomphe to the unusual Smoking Museum, with tips on where to shop and where to eat (from the expensive Tour d'Argent to the inexpensive Chartier).

If you have only a few days in Paris, we'll make it easy for you to truly experience the city instead of spending your time waiting in line at museums. Helpful walks through the most interesting areas of the city are included. You'll discover where the locals eat while avoiding tourist traps. In other words, you'll experience Paris like Parisians do.

Forget those large, bulky travel tomes. This handy little pocket guide to Paris is all you need to make your visit enjoyable, memorable—and easy.

1. SIGHTS

The Islands

Ile de la Cité

The Ile de la Cité is the birthplace of Paris. Surrounded by the Seine River, this island is home to Notre-Dame, la Ste-Chapelle and the Conciergerie.

Pont Neuf

1ⁱˢᵗ/Métro Pont Neuf

The twelve arches of the Pont Neuf connect the Ile de la Cité with both banks of the Seine River. Construction of this bridge began in 1578 and was completed in 1604.

Despite its name (which means "new bridge"), it's the oldest bridge in Paris. Pause here for a view of the Louvre Museum on the Right Bank and the beautiful apartments on the Left Bank.

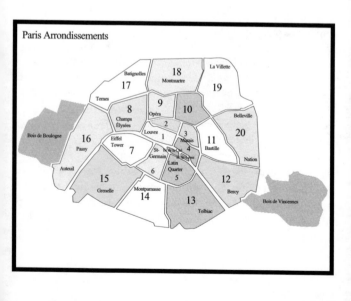

Paris Arrondissements

LEFT BANK VERSUS RIGHT BANK

Paris is divided into two parts by the Seine River. The Left Bank (*Rive Gauche*) is to the south and the Right Bank (*Rive Droite*) is to the north. When standing on a bridge over the Seine, if the water is flowing downstream, the Right Bank is to your right.

Les Bouquinistes

These little green stands along the Seine sell everything from replicas of the Eiffel Tower to old magazines. It's great fun to browse through French posters, postcards, and books. You can find inexpensive and interesting souvenirs. They open around 10 a.m. and close around 6 p.m. (except Sunday).

Musée de la Conciergerie
1ˢᵗ/Métro Cité
2 boulevard du Palais
Phone: 01/53.40.60.97
Open daily
Admission: 6€ adults, 4€ ages 18-25, under 18 free

The Conciergerie is a 14ᵗʰ century prison where over 2,600 people waited to have their heads chopped off, including Marie Antoinette, during the French Revolution's Reign of Terror.

It's a grim but interesting museum. The gothic palace that houses this museum along with the massive **Palais de Justice** were once part of the Palais de la Cité, the home of French kings. Today, the Palais de Justice houses the city's courts of law. You can watch the courts in session and view its beautiful interior for free. Closed Sun.

Ste-Chapelle
1ˢᵗ/Métro Cité
4 boulevard du Palais
Phone: 01/53.40.60.97
Open daily
Admission: 7€ adults, 4€ ages 18-25, under 18 free

On a sunny day, you'll be dazzled by nearly 6,600 square feet of stained glass at this Gothic masterpiece. The walls are made al-

PARIS MUSEUM PASS

If art is your passion but you don't want to wait in lines to see it, you can purchase a **Paris Museum Pass** and have access to over 70 museums and monuments, including the Louvre and Musée d'Orsay. The cost is 18€ for one day, 36€ for three days and 54€ for five days, and they're available at participating museums and many métro and bus stations.

most entirely of stained glass. The stained-glass windows owe their vibrant colors to the use of precious minerals and metals (gold for the red, cobalt for the blue). Fifteen windows depict biblical scenes from the Garden of Eden to the Apocalypse (the large rose window). The chapel was built in 1246 to house what some believe to be the Crown of Thorns, a nail from the crucifixion and other relics. It took less than two years to build, an amazing feat when one realizes that Notre-Dame took over two centuries to complete. On many evenings, especially in the summer, concerts are held here. Reservations for concerts can be made by calling 01/42.77.65.65.

place Louis-Lépine
4th/Métro Cité

On the north side of the island (Ile de la Cité) you'll find a lovely flower market (**Marché aux Fleurs**), but you may want to come here on Sundays when the market becomes a bird market (**Marché aux Oiseaux**) where all types of birds, supplies and cages are sold.

place du Parvis Notre-Dame
Admission: 3.50€ to the crypt, under 14 free. Crypt closed Mon.

The square in front of Notre-Dame is the center of all of France. A copper plaque on the ground outside the cathedral is **Point Zéro**

from which all distances in France are measured. Tradition holds that you'll be granted a wish if you stand on this point, close your eyes and turn three times. You'll also find the entry to the **Crypte Archéologique** here. In 1965, during construction of an underground parking garage, workers discovered ruins of Roman Paris. Today, you'll find a museum instead of a parking garage. To your left as you face the cathedral is the lovely exterior of the **Hôtel Dieu**, central Paris's main hospital. Pop into the main entrance and go straight ahead through the glass doors to view a beautiful French garden.

NO HALTER TOPS!
To gain entry to Notre-Dame and other churches in Paris, you'll need to dress appropriately. No halter tops, tank tops ... you get the picture. Guards will deny you entry if you aren't dressed appropriately.

Notre-Dame
4th/Métro Cité
6 place du Parvis Notre-Dame
Phone: 01/42.34.56.10
Open daily
Admission: Free to the cathedral. Towers: 6€, under 18 free. Treasury: 3€

Before construction of Notre-Dame began in 1163, the site

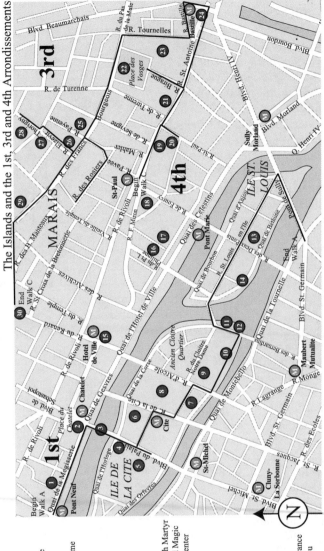

The Islands and the 1st, 3rd and 4th Arrondissements

1. Plant and Pet Market
2. Fountain of the Palms
3. Pont-au-Change
4. Musée de La Conciergerie
5. Ste-Chapelle
6. Place Louis-Lépine
7. Place du Parvis Notre-Dame
8. Hôtel Dieu
9. Notre-Dame
10. Square Jean XXIII
11. Square de l'Ile de France
12. Deportation Memorial
13. Ile St-Louis
14. Musée Mickiewicz
15. Hôtel de Ville
16. Museum Unknown Jewish Martyr
17. Museum of Curiosity and Magic
18. European Photography Center
19. Eglise St-Paul-St-Louis
20. Village St-Paul
21. Hôtel Sully
22. Place des Vosges
23. Victor Hugo's Home
24. Place de la Bastille
25. Musée Carnavalet
26. Musée Cognacq-Jay
27. Musée de la Serrure
28. Musée Picasso
29. Musée de l'Histoire de France
30. Centre Georges Pompidou
Ⓜ Métro Stop

was the home of a Roman temple to Jupiter, a Christian basilica, and a Romanesque church. Notre-Dame is one of the greatest achievements of Gothic architecture. Construction took nearly 200 years, and it has had a tumultuous history. Many treasures of the cathedral were destroyed at the end of the 18th century during the French Revolution. At one point, it was even used as a food warehouse.

On your right when you're facing the church is the statue of Charlemagne ("Charles the Great"). On the left doorway is St. Denis holding his head. He was the first martyr of France, decapitated by a jealous king for preaching Christianity. Legend has it that he picked up his head and walked to the village of St. Denis (head in hand) where he is now buried. In the center is Christ sitting on the Throne of Judgment with those damned to hell on the right in chains and those destined for heaven on the left. The twin towers are 226 feet high. You can climb the 387 steps of the north tower for a grand view of Paris. The famous gargoyles are found between the towers. The 295-foot-tall spire was added in 1860. Along the spire's base are apostles and evangelists (and the architect looking up to his spire). On the sides of the church are the famous "flying buttresses" (50-foot beams that support the Gothic structure).

The cathedral is so huge that it can accommodate over 6,000 visitors. The interior is dominated by three beautiful (and huge) rose windows and has a 7,800-pipe organ. Inside along the walls are individual chapels dedicated to saints. The most famous chapel is that of Joan of Arc in the right transept. The sacristy houses relics, manuscripts and religious garments. On Good Friday, what is said to be the Crown of Thorns and a piece of the cross on which Christ was crucified are put on public display. Events of note here include the crowning of Napoleon as emperor and the funeral of Charles de Gaulle.

Note: free organ recitals take place most Sunday afternoons.

Ancien Cloître Quartier
4th/Métro Cité
rue du Cloître-Notre-Dame north to quai des Fleurs on the Ile de la Cité (these streets are on the left side if you're facing the cathedral)

This area of six streets in the shadow of Notre-Dame is often overlooked. Medieval mansions make you feel like you've entered another era. Especially beautiful are rue Chanonesse, rue des Ursins and rue des Chantres.

Deportation Memorial
(Mémorial des Martyrs Français de la Déportation de 1945)
4th/Métro Cité
Open daily, but closed for several hours at lunch
Admission: Free

Easy to miss, this memorial behind Notre-Dame (at the easternmost point of the Ile de la Cité) reminds us to "Forgive, but don't forget." It was built in honor of the more than 30,000 citizens who were placed on boats at this spot for deportation to concentration camps.

You descend steps, become surrounded by walls, and then single-file enter a chamber. The plaque on the floor reads: "They descended into the mouth of the earth and they did not return." A hallway is covered with 200,000 lit crystals (one for each French citizen who died). At the far end of the hall is the eternal flame of hope. Don't miss this memorial. It's both moving and disturbing.

Square du Vert-Galant
4th/Métro Pont Neuf
This triangular square at the tip of the Ile de la Cité is down a flight of steps from the Pont Neuf and the statue of Henry IV. "Vert-Galant" means "old spark," the nickname for Henry IV, who was quite a ladies' man. It's a great place to see the Seine River and, appropriately, a favorite place for lovers.

Ile St-Louis
4th/Métro Pont Marie or Sully-Morland

You reach Ile St-Louis by crossing the footbridge behind Notre-Dame (Pont St-Louis). This charming residential island within the city is swamped with tourists during high season (especially the rue St-Louis-en-l'Ile, the main avenue). The vast majority of the buildings date back to the 1600s, making for a beautiful place to stroll, especially the small side streets. There are interesting shops and several good restaurants.

Musée Adam Mickiewicz
4th/Métro Pont Marie
6 quai d'Orléans
Phone: 01/43.54.35.61
Open Thursdays
Admission: 6€

Everything Polish at the only museum on the Ile St-Louis. Adam Mickiewicz was a poet and political activist. It houses his works, paintings and sculpture of 19th- and 20th-century Polish artists and a separate section, the **Salle Chopin**, devoted to the manuscripts and personal belongings of Chopin.

1st and 2nd Arrondissements

The 1st is the center of Paris where many tourist attractions are found, including the Louvre, Palais Royal and Jardin des Tuileries. The adjoining 2nd is primarily a business district.

> ### WHAT IS AN ARRONDISSEMENT?
> Paris is divided into 20 arrondissements or districts. Each arrondissement has a city hall, police station, post office and mayor. See map on page 8.

Jardin des Tuileries
1st/Métro Tuileries or Concorde
West of the Louvre to the place de la Concorde

The same man who planned the gardens of Versailles designed the Tuileries. The garden takes its name from the word *tuil* or tile (roof-tile factories once were here). You'll enjoy bubbling fountains, statues, flowers and trees between the Louvre and place de la Concorde. Sit down and relax in this beautiful garden in the middle of Paris.

Musée de l'Orangerie des Tuileries
1st/Métro Concorde
West end of Jardin des Tuileries at 1 place de la Concorde
Phone: 01/42.60.69.69
Closed Tues.
Admission: 6€

This former 19th-century greenhouse is situated in the beautiful Tuileries garden and is the home of the Impressionist art collection of Jean Walter and Paul Guillaume. The art was sold to France by Domenica Walter (who was married to both men).

The collection numbers 143 paintings from the late nineteenth century and the first half of the twentieth century (including 15 Cézannes, 24 Renoirs, 10 Matisses and 12 Picassos). Of particular note are the eight large *Water Lilies* that Monet gave France in 1922.

While visiting the Louvre can be overwhelming (so many paintings, so little time), the Orangerie is small and manageable. After years of renovation, the Orangerie is reopening in 2005.

1st, 2nd, 3rd, 9th and 10th Arrondissements

1. Jardin des Tuileries
2. Musée National du Louvre
3. Palais Royal
4. Eglise St-Roch
5. Place Vendôme
6. Galerie Vivienne
7. Place des Victoires
8. Bourse du Commerce
9. Forum des Halles
10. Musée du Barreau de Paris
11. Eglise St-Eustache
12. Musée des Arts et Métiers
13. Opéra Garnier
14. Paris-Story
15. Musée de la Parfumerie-Fragonard
16. Drouot-Richelieu Auctions
17. Grévin Wax Museum
18. Passage des Panoramas
19. Bourse (Stock Exchange)
20. Passage Brady
21. Musée Gustave-Moreau
22. Grande Synagogue de la Victoire
23. Musée du Grand Orient de France
24. Pinacothèque de Paris
25. Canal St-Martin

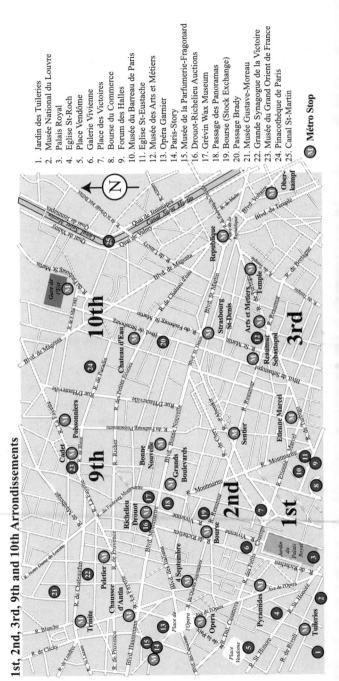

Métro Stop

Galerie Nationale du Jeu de Paume
1st/Métro Concorde
Northeast corner of the Jardin des Tuileries at 1 place de la Concorde
Phone: 01/47.03.12.50
Closed Mon.
Admission: 6€, under 13 free

Named after a ball game similar to tennis that was played here, this museum was used to house a huge Impressionist collection (now at the Musée d'Orsay). Today, it serves as the gallery for temporary exhibits that change every two to three months. It now houses the **Galerie Nationale de l'Image** (the national video and photography museum).

place des Pyramides
1st/Métro Tuileries

This square is home to a glistening gold equestrian statue of Joan of Arc.

place Vendôme
1st/Métro Tuileries
Between the Jardin des Tuileries and the Opéra Garnier

This elegant square is the home of a 144-foot column honoring Napoleon. The column is faced with bronze from 1,200 melted cannons from Austrian and Russian armies. That's Napoleon on top dressed as Julius Caesar. Although the Ministry of Justice is here, most notice the luxury Ritz Hotel and the expensive shops nearby, especially on rue St-Honoré. You'll find world-famous jewelers here, and great shopping for those with lots of disposable income.

Eglise St-Roch
1st/Métro Tuileries
296 rue St-Honoré
Phone: 01/42.44.13.20
Open daily
Admission: Free

Designed by the same architect who designed the Louvre, this church houses religious artifacts from ancient monasteries and churches. Notice its richly decorated dome. Marks of Napoleon's 1795 attack on royalist troops who were defending the church can be seen on the outside.

RESTAURANT TIP
Le Soufflé
1ˢᵗ/Métro Tuileries
36 rue du Mont-Thabor
(between places Vendôme and Concorde)
Phone: 01/42.60.27.19
Fax: 01/42.60.54.98
Closed Sun.

The name is deceiving as this restaurant, known for its *soufflés*, has a full menu. It has become quite touristy, but diners praise the service. Moderate. �֍

Bourse
2ⁿᵈ/Métro Bourse
4 place de la Bourse
Phone: 01/49.27.55.52
Open weekday afternoons
Admission: 5€

The French stock exchange is a lot more sedate than Wall Street, and you'll need your passport to get in. Tours are only in French. The stock exchange is housed in an 1800s Romanesque temple. How French!

places des Victoires
1ˢᵗ/Métro Bourse or Sentier

Laid out in 1685 to honor the military victories of Louis XIV, this circular square is now where you come to buy-or gawk at-top fashion boutiques. That's Louis XIV galloping on his horse in the middle of the square.

SHOPPING TIP
Galerie Vivienne
2ⁿᵈ/Métro Bourse
4 rue des Petits-Champs
Open daily

Duck into this elegant and beautiful gallery of luxurious shops. While here, check out **Legrand Filles et Fils**, Phone: 01/42.60.07.12. This wine shop and bar has been run by the Legrand family for over three generations. Be sure to check out the cork-covered ceiling. The gallery leads into the **Galerie Colbert**. ✥

Palais Royal
1ˢᵗ/Métro Palais-Royal
place Palais Royal (across the rue de Rivoli from the Louvre)

The Palais Royal was built in 1632. It now houses ministries of the French government (so you won't be able to look inside). You come here to take a break in the calm, beautiful garden. The buildings around the garden, built in the 1700s, are home to everything from stamp shops to art galleries. If you're interested in sculpture, check out the controversial (meaning some did not like it) 280 prison-striped columns by Daniel Buren that were placed in the main courtyard. Very 80s!

RESTAURANT TIP
Le Grand Colbert
2nd/Métro Bourse
2 rue Vivienne (near the place des Victoires)
Phone: 01/42.86.87.88
Fax: 01/42.86.82.65
Closed part of Aug.

Housed in a restored historic building, serving traditional *brasserie* cuisine. Known for its seafood tray. This restaurant was featured in the 2003 movie *Something's Gotta Give*. Moderate. ✻

Musée National du Louvre
1st/Métro Palais-Royal
34-36 quai du Louvre
Phone: 01/40.20.53.17 (recorded message)
Closed Tues.
Admission: 8.50€, (6€ after 6 p.m. on Mon. and Wed). Thurs.

RESTAURANT TIP
Aux Lyonnais
2nd/Métro Bourse
32 rue St-Marc
Phone: 01/42.96.65.04
Fax: 01/42.97.42.95
Closed Sun. and Mon. (lunch)

Parisians have always found that what was once old is now new. Such is the case with this beautiful century-old bistro, which has been recently renovated and serves the cuisine of Lyon. The wine of choice is Beaujolais. Moderate.✻

- Sun. 9 a.m.-6 p.m. Mon and Wed 9 a.m.-9:45 p.m. Free the first Sunday of the month. 8.50€ for exhibitions in Napoléon Hall. www.louvre.fr

Note: It's quicker if you enter through the Carrousel du Louvre mall at 99 rue de Rivoli rather than through the glass pyramid. The Louvre is open late on Monday and Wednesday and is usually least crowded in the afternoon.

Simply put, the Louvre is the greatest art museum in the world. With that said, if you have only a short stay in Paris, don't try to conquer the crowded museum at the expense of seeing the rest of Paris. It's huge. It's the largest art museum in the world, the largest building in Paris, and it's in the largest palace in Europe.

The buildings that house the Louvre were constructed in the 13th century as a fortress. Today, the inner courtyard is the site of the controversial (but I think, fantastic) glass pyramid that serves as the main entrance to the museum. The pyramid, designed by the famous architect I.M. Pei, is a brilliant entry to the museum.

You'll find some of the following famous pieces of art (of the 30,000 here) at the Louvre:

• Leonardo da Vinci's *La Gioconda* (the *Mona Lisa*), *Virgin and Child with Saint Anne* and *Virgin of the Rocks*

• Michelangelo's *Esclaves* (*Slaves*) Titian's *Open Air Concert* Raphael's *La Belle Jardinière* Veronese's *Wedding Feast at Cana*

• Not to mention the *Venus de Milo*, *Winged Victory*...

It really doesn't matter what you see and what you don't see. Just the experience of viewing so much famous art in one place is alone worth the trip to Paris.

Here's what the Louvre has in store from top to bottom:

Second Floor:
Northern European paintings, drawings and prints; 14th- to 19th-century French paintings; and 17th-century French drawings and prints.

First Floor:
Italian-school paintings and drawings; Italian paintings (including the *Mona Lisa*); 19th-century large French paintings; Egyptian, Greek, Etruscan and Roman antiquities; and *objets d'art*.

Ground Floor:
16th- to 19th-century Italian sculptures; Islamic, Asia Minor, Egyptian, Greek, Etruscan and Roman antiquities (including *Venus de Milo*); Middle Ages and Renaissance French sculptures; and 17th- to 19th-century French and Northern European sculptures.

RESTAURANT TIP
Café Marly
1st/Métro Musée du Louvre/ Palais-Royal
93 rue de Rivoli
Phone: 01/49.26.06.60

Hungry after all that art? This café overlooks the pyramid at the Louvre and is popular with visitors to the museum. The setting makes up for any complaints about the "ordinary" food. Moderate. ❧

Below Ground Floor:
11th- to 15th-century Italian sculptures; Medieval Art; Islamic Art; Greek antiquities; and 17th- and 18th-century French sculptures.

SHOPPING TIP
Le Carrousel du Louvre
1st/Métro Palais-Royal
99 rue de Rivoli
Closed Tues.

Had it with art? How about looking at some consumer goods? You'll find a shopping mall with over 30 stores below the Louvre. There's also a restaurant court here. An inverted glass pyramid drops down into the center of the mall. Look familiar? It was also designed by I.M. Pei, who designed the famous pyramid entry to the Louvre. Another nearby shopping diversion is **Le Webstore**, 2nd/Métro Louvre, 29 rue du Louvre, Phone: 01/40.26.92.77. This interesting store sells everything from flashlights to T-shirts to electronic gadgets.

Rue de Rivoli
The rue de Rivoli links the Louvre with the Champs-Élysées. Commissioned by Napoleon for victory marches, it's named after his victory over the Austrians at Rivoli in 1797. He never stepped foot on this street as it was not completed until the mid-1800s, long after his death. There are beautiful arcades with neo-Classical apartments above them. Today, the arcades house a mixture of souvenir and luxury goods shops.

Arc du Carrousel
1st/Métro Palais-Royal

A small triumphal arch, topped with four bronze horses, between the Louvre and the Tuileries.

Musée des Arts Décoratifs
1st/Métro Palais-Royal or Tuileries
107 rue de Rivoli
Phone: 01/44.55.57.50
Closed Mon.
Admission: 6€, 4.50€ ages 18-25, under 18 free

Wallpaper, furniture, fabric and other decorations from the 17th century to the present are found in this special-interest museum (especially for those who are fans of Art Deco) located in the Palais du Louvre. There are Medieval, Renaissance, Art Nouveau and Art Deco rooms. There's also a **Museum of Advertising (Musée de la Publicité)** which chronicles the history of advertising from 18th-century posters to modern-day advertising.

Musée de la Mode et du Textile
1st/Métro Palais-Royal or Tuileries
107 rue de Rivoli
Phone: 01/44.55.57.50
Closed Mon.
Admission: 6€, 4.50€ ages 18-25, under 18 free

This museum, in the Palais du Louvre, houses one of the largest collections of garments, accessories and textiles from the 17th century to the present. A must for those interested in fashion.

St-Germain-l'Auxerrois
1st/Métro Louvre-Rivoli
2 place du Louvre
Phone: 01/42.60.13.96
Open daily
Admission: Free

This beautiful Gothic church, with its gruesome gargoyles, incredible stained glass and beautiful carved wood pews, make it worth a visit. At the stroke of midnight on August 24, 1572, the bells of this church signaled the massacre of three thousand Protestants. The king ordered the massacre because of rumors that the Protestants were going to kill him.

Forum des Halles
1st/Métro Les Halles

Unattractive, underground mall (and métro and bus station) where Paris's youth hang out in droves. Chain stores, a swimming pool and movie-theatre complex are all here. Skip it! The park above, with its Renaissance fountain, the **Fontaine des Innocents**, is quite nice.

WINE BARS

Parisians love wine bars and so should you. Two great wine bars are:

Willi's Wine Bar
1st/Métro Bourse
13 rue des Petits-Champs
Phone: 01/42.61.05.09
Fax: 01/47.03.36.93
Closed Sun.

British owners serving Parisian specialties. A great wine list and a favorite of many travelers to Paris. Moderate.

Juvenile's
1st/Métro Bourse
47 rue de Richelieu
Phone: 01/42.97.46.49
Fax: 01/42.60.31.52
Closed Sun.

Around the corner from Willi's Wine Bar, this unpretentious wine bar serves light meals and has a large wine selection. Friendly and fun. Inexpensive – Moderate. ✤

SHOPPING TIP
A. Simon
2nd/Métro Les Halles
48 rue Montmartre
Phone: 01/42.33.71.65
Closed Sun. and Mon.

This kitchenware shop is where the chefs shop. You can fill your own kitchen with pans, glassware and some stuff you find only in bistros (like paper doilies).

Eglise St-Eustache
1st/Métro Les Halles
2 rue du Jour
Phone: 01/42.36.31. 05
Open daily
Admission: Free

This beautiful Gothic and Renaissance church dates back to 1532. Rembrandt's *Pilgrimage to Emmaus* is here along with John Armleder's modern *Pour Paintings* that were added to the church in 2000. The church hosts contemporary art exhibits and occasional organ concerts featuring the ornate and immense pipe organ.

It's a tradition in the Catholic church to light a candle and say a prayer for an "intention." Candles of all sizes and costs are found in nearly all churches, although some have tacky electric candles. Slip a coin or bill into the slot, pick a candle, light it and pray that next time you'll have more time to spend in Paris.

Bourse du Commerce
1st/Métro Les Halles
rue de Viarmes

Originally the Corn Exchange, this circular, domed 18th-century building is the Commercial Exchange for France.

ENTERTAINMENT TIP
Jazz Clubs on rue des Lombards
Parisians love jazz. There are several jazz clubs on rue des Lombards (1st/ Métro Châtelet or Les Halles). They are usually smoky and nothing gets going until after 9 p.m. (if then). Take your pick:

Au Duc des Lombards, 42 rue des Lombards (modern jazz).

Le Saiser Salé, 58 rue des Lombards (fusion, funk, salsa).

Le Sunset, 60 rue des Lombards (fusion).

Le Sunside, 60 rue des Lombards (traditional jazz and swing).

Musée du Barreau de Paris
1ˢᵗ/Métro Les Halles
25 rue du Jour
Phone: 01/47.83.50.03
Group visits only
Admission: Free

Devoted to the history of French law, this museum is often included on lawyers' group tours to Paris. Imagine how fun traveling with a bunch of lawyers would be! I can say that. I'm a lawyer.

Passages
2ⁿᵈ/Métro Grands Boulevards

In the 1800s, there were 137 glass-roofed shopping arcades (*passages*). Only 24 remain. The oldest, dating back to 1800, is **Passage des Panoramas**, 11 blvd. Montmartre

(known for its stamps). Nearby are **Passage Verdeau**, 4-6 rue de la Grange Batelière and **Passage Jouffroy**, 12 blvd. Montmartre. *Passages* are luminous and practical. The glass roofs not only admit light, but they shelter shoppers from rain.

> **FOOD ON THE RUN TIP**
> Stohrer
> *2ⁿᵈ/Métro Les Halles*
> *51 rue Montorgueil*
> *Phone: 01/42.33.38.20*
> *Closed part of Aug.*
>
> The delicious Parisian favorite of *baba au rhum* (spongecake soaked in rum) was invented at this (*pâtisserie*) bakery. Stop in!

3ʳᵈ and 4ᵗʰ Arrondissements

The Marais is comprised of roughly the 3ʳᵈ and 4ᵗʰ arrondissements on the Right Bank. This area, with its small streets and beautiful squares, is filled with interesting shops. It's home to both a thriving Jewish community and a large gay community. It's considered the "cœur historique," historic heart of Paris, and has retained some of the flavor of the French Renaissance.

Hôtel de Ville
4ᵗʰ/Métro Hôtel de Ville
rue de Rivoli at the place de l'Hôtel de Ville

No, it's not a hotel, it's the City Hall of Paris. Splendid, ornate and overlooking the Seine River, it's mostly closed to the public (guided tours only), but is certainly worth a look from the large fountained square in front. You'll find a large skating rink here in the winter and a beach for volley-ball in the summer. Art and cultural exhibits are held here at 5 rue de Lobau (Salle St-Jean) and 29 rue de Rivoli (Salon d'Accueil).

CHRISTMAS IN PARIS!
A skating rink is installed in front of the Hôtel de Ville. The large windows of the major department stores (Bon Marché, BHV, Galeries Lafayette, La Samaritaine and Printemps) are decorated in interesting (or strange?) Christmas themes. One of the best ways to experience Christmas in Paris is to walk around the following areas decorated with beautiful lights: Avenue des Champs-Élysées, Rue du Faubourg- St-Honoré, Rue de Castiglione, Quartier Montmartre, place des Victoires, place Vendôme, Avenue Montaigne, Rue Montorgueil, Rue des Petits-Carreaux and Rue de la Paix. ❧

Tour St-Jacques
4th/Métro Châtelet or Hôtel de Ville
Square de la Tour St-Jacques (between rue de Rivoli and avenue Victoria)

The flamboyant Gothic bell tower dating back to 1523 is all that remains of the church of St-

Jacques, which was destroyed during the Revolution.

St-Gervais-St-Protais
4th/Métro Hôtel de Ville
place St-Gervais (near rue François Miron)
Phone: 01/47.26.78.38 (concert information)
Closed Mon.
Admission: Free

A site of frequent choral and organ concerts, this church near the Hôtel de Ville is named after two Roman soldiers who were martyred by Emperor Nero. The Gothic church is known for its acoustics and decorated columns.

Museum of Jewish Art and History
(Musée d'Art et d'Histoire du Judaïsme)
3rd/Métro Rambuteau
71 rue du Temple
Phone: 01/53.01.86.60
Closed Sat.
Admission: 7€, under 18 free

Located in the 17th-century **Hôtel de St-Aignan**, this museum not only has a collection of Jewish religious artifacts, but also artwork by famous Jewish painters, including Chagall. Exhibitions are devoted to Jewish culture in Paris and throughout Europe.

Centre Georges Pompidou
4th/Métro Rambuteau

place Georges-Pompidou (on rue St-Martin between rue Rambuteau and rue St-Merri)
Phone: 01/44.78.12.33
Closed Tues.
Admission: To the Center: 10€, 8€ ages 13-25, under 13 free. To the exhibits: 9€ or 7€ (depending on the exhibit), 7€ or 5€ ages 13-25, under 13 free. To the Modern Art Museum only: 7€, 5€ ages 18-25, under 18 free

Named after Georges Pompidou, president of France 1969-1974, this museum of 20th- and 21st-century art is a must-see. The building is a work of art in itself. Opened in 1977, the controversial building is "ekoskeletal" (the plumbing, elevators, and ducts all are exposed and brightly painted). The ducts are color coded: blue for air conditioning, green for water, yellow for electricity, and red for transportation. Parisians call this "Beaubourg" after the neighborhood in which it's located. **The National Museum of Modern Art** (Musée National d'Art Moderne), the **Institute for Research and Coordination of Acoustics/Music** (Institut de Recherche et de Coordination Acoustique-Musique) and the **Public Library** (Bibliothèque Information Publique) are all here. The Modern Art museum has works by Picasso, Matisse, Kandinsky, Pollock and many other favorite modern artists. There's a great view from the rooftop restaurant (Georges). The **Stravinsky Fountain** and its moving mobile sculptures and circus atmosphere are found just to the south of the museum. Check out the red pouty lips in the fountain!

RESTAURANT TIP
Café Beaubourg
4th/Métro Rambuteau
100 rue St-Martin
Phone: 01/48.87.63.96

Looking onto the Centre Pompidou and packed with an artsy crowd. Recommended for a drink and perhaps a snack. The food is not that great, but the bathrooms are worth the trip. Moderate. ✻

Quartier des Horloges
3rd/Métro Rambuteau
Quartier des Horloges (off of rue Beaubourg)
Near the Rambuteau métro stop

Hidden in this small, modern courtyard (hanging from a wall) is the brass sculpture *The Defender of Time*. Each hour, a knight does battle with a dragon, crab or bird (representing earth, water and air). At noon, 6 p.m. and 10 p.m., he does battle with all three!

Doll Museum
(Musée de la Poupée)
3rd/Métro Rambuteau
Impasse Berthaud (off of rue Beaubourg)
Phone: 01/42.72.55.90
Closed Mon. and Tues.
Admission: 6€, 4€ ages 3-18, under 3 free

A museum displaying over 200 dolls produced in France from the 1800s to today. There's also a gift shop for all doll lovers.

RESTAURANT TIP
Le Hangar
3rd/Métro Rambuteau
12 impasse Berthaud (off of rue Beaubourg)
Phone: 01/42.74.55.44
Closed dates vary. No credit cards.

Nothing fancy about this bistro near the Pompidou Center. Good food at reasonable prices. Excellent chocolate cake. Inexpensive. ❊

La Maison du Haut-Pignon
(3rd/Métro Rambuteau)
51 rue Montmorency

Why are Harry Potter fans looking at the oldest building in Paris? **La Maison du Haut-Pignon** was built in 1407. Nicolas Flamel (the alchemist whose sorcerer's stone is the source of immortality in Harry Potter books) used to live here. Today, a restaurant (**Auberge Nicolas Flamel**) occupies the premises.

Eglise St-Merri
4th/Métro Métro Hôtel de Ville or Rambuteau
78 rue St-Martin (at rue de la Verrerie)
Phone: 01/42.71.40.75 (for concerts)
Open daily
Admission: Free

This church dates from the mid-16th century and has a flamboyant Gothic exterior (including lots of gargoyles). Its interior isn't so bad either. Lots of stained glass and a famous wooden organ. The composer Saint-Saëns was once an organist here. The church bell is said to be the oldest in Paris.

ENTERTAINMENT TIP
A Little Bit of Ireland in Paris
Many Irish live in Paris. Irish pubs are popular not only with the Irish who are looking for a pint, but also with Parisians. Most Irish pubs feature live music (especially on the weekends). A favorite is **Quiet Man** at 5 rue des Haudriettes, *3rd/Métro Rambuteau*, Phone: 01/48.04.42.77. ❊

Musée des Arts et Métiers
3rd/Métro Arts et Métiers
60 rue Réaumur
Phone: 01/53.01.82.00
Closed Mon.
Admission: 6.50€, under 18 free

A huge interactive museum of science and industry. It's located in the former church of St-Martin des Champs.

> **SHOPPING TIP**
> Budget name-brand shoes? You'll find last season's shoe collections at the crowded discount stores on **rue Meslay** in the République area. *3rd/Métro* République. ✼

> **RESTAURANT TIP**
> Au Bascou
> *3rd/Métro Arts-et-Métiers*
> *38 rue Réaumur*
> *Phone: 01/42.72.69.25*
> *Fax: 01/42.72.69.25*
> *Closed Sat. (lunch), Sun., Mon. (lunch), and Aug.*
>
> Modern bistro near the place de la République serving Basque specialties. *Piperade* (a spicy omelet) is the specialty. Moderate. ✼

Promenades Gourmandes
3rd/Métro Temple
187 Rue du Temple
Phone: 01/48.04.56.84
Admission: Classes are held Tue-Fri. $200 for a half-day session, $290 for a full-day session which includes a gourmet walking tour

Paule Caillat, who speaks fluent English, operates her unique business from her apartment. Groups of six (mostly Americans) meet her at a café, visit a market to purchase ingredients for lunch, and then head to her apartment to cook a meal. It's a truly hands-on and 'mouth-full' experience.

> **RESTAURANT TIP**
> Chez Jenny
> *3rd/Métro République*
> *39 boulevard du Temple*
> *Phone: 01/44.54.39.00*
>
> A little bit of the Alsace region of France can be found in this *brasserie* on the place de la République. Hope you like *choucroute* (sauerkraut). Moderate. ✼

Musée de l'Histoire de France/ Musée des Archives Nationales
3rd/Métro Hôtel de Ville
60 rue des Francs-Bourgeois
Phone: 01/40.27.60.96
Closed Tues.
Admission: 3€, under 18 free

This museum has France's most

famous documents including those written by Joan of Arc, Marie Antoinette and Napoleon. It's located in the **Hôtel de Clisson**, a palace dating back to 1371, the highlight of which is the incredibly ornate, oval-shaped **Salon Ovale**.

SHOPPING TIP

Les Touristes

4th/Métro Hôtel-de-Ville or Rambuteau

17 rue des Blancs-Manteaux

Phone: 01/42.72.10.84

Closed Sun.

You can always find something unusual at this Marais boutique filled with interesting things the owners have collected during their trips around the world. Great place to buy gifts to bring home. ✄

Hunting Museum

(Musée de la Chasse et de la Nature)

3rd/Métro Hôtel-de-Ville

60 rue des Archives

Phone: 01/53.01.92.40

Closed Mon.

Admission: 5€. Under 4 free

A must for hunters and those interested in guns. This museum is located in a Marais mansion and includes paintings of hunting scenes, firearms dating back to the 17th century, and hunting trophies.

Musée Picasso

3rd/Métro St-Sébastien or St-Paul

5 rue de Thorigny

Phone: 01/42.71.25.21

Closed Tues.

Admission: 5.50€, 4€ ages 18-25, under 18 free. 4€ on Sun. and free the first Sun. of the month

Often crowded, this museum, housed in a 17th-century mansion, has the largest Picasso collection in the world. The collection was given to the French government in lieu of death taxes. There are 1,500 drawings, 230 paintings and over 1,600 prints (not to mention works by Renoir, Cézanne, Degas and Matisse). There's also a large collection of African masks that Picasso collected. Although there are no "masterpieces" here, this is a fine collection from every period of Picasso's artistic life. This museum is located in the beautifully restored **Hôtel Salé**, which was built in the mid-1600s. The owner was a salt-tax collector (*salé* means "salty").

Musée de la Serrure/Musée Bricard

3rd/Métro St-Paul

1 rue de la Perle (at the intersection of rue de Thorigny)

Phone: 01/42.77.79.62

Closed mornings and Sat. and Sun.

Admission: 5€

From Roman times to the present, this special-interest museum celebrates the art of the locksmith. It's located in the small and lovely **Hôtel Libéral Bruant**, an Italianate mansion.

Musée Cognacq-Jay
3ʳᵈ/Métro St-Paul
8 rue Elzévir
Phone: 01/40.27.07.21
Closed Mon.
Admission: Free

This free museum in the Marais houses the 18ᵗʰ-century art and furniture owned by Ernest Cognacq, the founder of La Samaritaine department store. Works by Rembrandt, Fragonard, Boucher and others are here in this quiet museum located in the **Hôtel Donon**, an elegant mansion. Cognacq once bragged that he was not a lover of art and that he had never visited the Louvre. Perhaps it was his wife, Louise Jay, who had the sense to compile such an amazing art collection.

Musée Carnavalet-Histoire de Paris
3ʳᵈ/Métro St-Paul
23 rue de Sévigné
Phone: 01/44.59.58.58.
Closed Mon.
Admission: Permanent collection is free. 6€ for exhibits

In the 1700s, the Hôtel Carnavalet was presided over by Madame de Sévigné who chronicled French society in hundreds of letters written to her daughter. I went kicking and screaming into this museum as it sounded so very boring. I was wrong. You'll find antiques, portraits, and artifacts dating back to the late 1700s. Did I mention that it's free? The section on the French Revolution with its guillotines is especially interesting as is the royal bedroom. There are exhibits across the courtyard at the **Hôtel le Peletier de St-Fargeau**. Truly an interesting museum of the history of Paris.

Memorial to the Unknown Jewish Martyr (Memorial du Martyr Juif Inconnu)
4ᵗʰ/Métro St-Paul
17 rue Geoffroy-l'Asnier
Phone: 01/42.77.44.72
Closed Sat.
Admission: 3€

On a small side street not far from the St-Paul métro, this stark memorial is dedicated to the six million Jews who died during

World War II. The crypt has a black-marble Star of David containing the ashes of concentration camp victims. There's a research and document center, and a museum that displays photos and documents on the Holocaust.

European Photography Center (Maison Européenne de la Photographie)
4th/Métro St-Paul
5-7 rue de Fourcy
Phone: 01/44.78.75.00
Closed. Mon and Tues.
Admission: 5€

Displays works by contemporary photographers (both European and American) in modern galleries.

Hôtel Sully
4th/Métro St-Paul
62 rue St-Antoine

This mansion in the French Renaissance style has a beautiful garden and courtyard open to the public. The **Caisse Nationale des Monuments Historiques** (the headquarters for administering France's historic monuments) is located here. There's an excellent bookstore with an English section selling books about Paris.

Eglise St-Paul-St-Louis
4th/Métro St-Paul
101 rue St-Antoine (near rue St-Paul)
Admission: Free

This Baroque church (the Jesuit church in Paris) has a huge dome dating back to the 1600s. Of note is the Delacroix painting *Christ on the Mount of Olives*, and the shell-shaped holy-water fonts (donated by Victor Hugo who attended mass here).

Village St-Paul
4th/Métro St-Paul
23-27 rue St-Paul

An attractive passageway with cobblestone courtyards and interesting shops, especially antique shops. If you walk to the end of the courtyard and cross the little street, you can see vestiges of a wall built by Philippe Auguste in the 13th century. This wall surrounded Paris and was meant to protect it from hostile invasions.

RESTAURANT TIP
L'Enoteca
4th/Métro St-Paul
25 rue Charles V
Phone: 01/42.78.91.44
Fax: 01/44.59.31.72

Attractive Italian wine bar/bistro in the Marais. It has one of the largest Italian wine selections in Paris. Moderate. ❧

Museum of Curiosity and Magic/Academy of Magic (Musée de la Curiosité et de la Magie/Académie de la Magie)
4th/Métro St-Paul
11 rue St-Paul
Phone: 01/42.72.13.26
Open Wed., Sat. and Sun.
Admission: 7€

This museum (great for kids) is located in rooms made to look like caves. It's filled with over 3,000 magic props (like an early sawing-a-person-in-half box, trick cards and vibrating tables). Tours are in English and French. A live magic show is included.

place des Vosges
4th/Métro St-Paul or Bastille
Enter rue de Birague (off of rue St-Antoine)

Simply the most beautiful square in Paris, in France, and probably all of Europe. It's the oldest square in Paris, a beautiful and quiet park surrounded by stone and red-brick houses. Upscale boutiques are found in the attractive arcades. The square is also known as la place Royale as it was designed for royal festivities. Don't miss it!

Victor Hugo's Home (Maison de Victor Hugo)
4th/Métro St-Paul or Bastille
6 place des Vosges
Phone: 01/42.72.10.16

Closed Mon.
Admission: 6€

You can't seem to go anywhere in this city without seeing the name of Victor Hugo (he wrote *Les Miserables* and *The Hunchback of Notre Dame*). This 19th-century literary legend's home is

---

FOOD ON THE RUN TIP
In the heart of the Jewish community of the Marais are these two **Jewish delis:**

Jo Goldenberg
4th/Métro St-Paul
7 rue des Rosiers
Phone: 01/48.87.20.16
Fax: 01/42.78.15.29

Jo Goldenberg became famous for the wrong reason (the bombing by anti-Semitic terrorists in the early 1980s). Take-out and restaurant. Inexpensive.

Chez Marianne
4th/Métro St-Paul
2 rue des Hospitalières-St-Gervais
Phone: 01/42.72.18.86

Popular, charming take-away deli (you can also eat here) known for their authentic Jewish specialties. Inexpensive. ❧

now a museum. Hugo was also an artist, and you can view 350 of his drawings here.

RESTAURANT TIP
Ma Bourgogne
4th/Métro St-Paul or Bastille
19 place des Vosges.
Phone: 01/42.78.44.64

This café/restaurant in the place des Vosges serves traditional Parisian cuisine and specializes in roast chicken. Moderate. ✲

RESTAURANT TIP
Bofinger
4th/Métro Bastille
5 rue de la Bastille
Phone: 01/42.72.87.82
Fax: 01/42.72.97.68
Open until 1 a.m.

Beautiful glass-roofed *brasserie*, with lots of stained glass and brass, located between the place des Vosges and the place de la Bastille. It's the oldest Alsatian *brasserie* in Paris and still serves traditional dishes like *choucroute* (sauerkraut) and large platters of shellfish. Across the street and less expensive is **Le Petit Bofinger**, 6 rue de la Bastille, Phone: 01/42.72.05.23. Moderate. ✲

5th Arrondissement

The 5th, south of Ile de la Cité on the Left Bank of the Seine, is home to the **Latin Quarter**. It's a maze of small streets and squares surrounding **La Sorbonne**, the famous university. The name Latin Quarter comes from the university tradition of speaking and studying in Latin.

place St-Michel
5th/ Métro St-Michel
End of boulevard St-Michel at the Seine River

This much-photographed square is filled with tourists and locals. It's dominated by the ornate fountain and statue of Michael, the archangel, defeat-

1. Square du Vert-Galant
2. Pont-au-Change
3. Musée de La Conciergerie
4. Ste-Chapelle
5. Place Louis-Lépine
6. Place du Parvis Notre-Dame
7. Hôtel Dieu
8. Notre-Dame
9. Square Jean XXIII
10. Square de l'Ile de France
11. Deportation Memorial
12. Ile St-Louis
13. Musée National du Louvre
14. Musée d'Orsay
15. Institut de France
16. Musée de la Monnaie
17. Place St-Michel
18. St-Séverin
19. St-Julien-le-Pauvre
20. Square René-Viviani
21. Anatomy Museum
22. Eglise St-Germain-des-Prés
23. Musée Delacroix
24. Place Fürstenberg
25. Cour du Commerce
26. Musée de Cluny
27. Place de la Sorbonne
28. St-Sulpice
29. Museum of Medical History
30. Police Museum
Métro Stop

5th and 6th Arrondissements

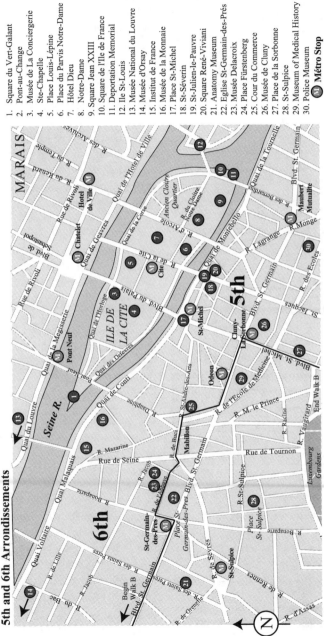

ing Lucifer. It's also the site of a memorial to the liberation of France in 1944.

St-Séverin
5th/Métro St-Michel
rue des Prêtres-St-Séverin
Open daily
Admission: Free

Built in the early 1200s, this flamboyant Gothic church has one of the most interesting roofs with gargoyles, monsters and birds of prey. The interior, with its beautiful pillars and stained glass depicting the seven sacraments, isn't bad either.

> **GO TO A CONCERT!**
> You'll see posters all over advertising choral or orchestra concerts at bargain prices. Usually, these concerts are held in beautiful, but lesser-known churches throughout Paris and make for a wonderful evening before dinner. ❧

St-Julien-le-Pauvre
5th/Métro St-Michel
rue St-Julien-le-Pauvre
Open daily
Admission: Free

This church is named after St. Julien. He was called "Le Pauvre" (the poor) because he gave all his money away. This small church is also the oldest in Paris, dating back to 1170. It's now a Greek Orthodox church.

Square René-Viviani
5th/Métro St-Michel
Off of the quai de Montebello

This attractive square has one of the best views of Notre-Dame across the river. The oldest tree in Paris (brought here as a seedling from French Guiana in South America in 1680) is here. You can't miss it. It's the one with the wooden supports holding it up. Notice the green-painted fountain. At the end of the 19th century, an English art collector, Richard Wallace, donated hundreds of these fountains to the city. He thought it was unfair that there was nowhere in Paris that you could get a free glass of water (you had to pay for it in a café).

Shakespeare and Company
5th/Métro St-Michel
37 rue de la Bûcherie
Phone: 01/43.26.96.50
Open daily

This famous bookstore is named after the publishing house that first released James Joyce's *Ulysses*. Hemingway and Fitzgerald were patrons. It's a favorite hangout for expatriates from English-speaking countries. Poetry readings on Monday evenings (if you like that

RESTAURANT TIPS
FOR THE LATIN QUARTER
La Maison
5th/Métro St-Michel
1 rue de la Bûcherie
Phone: 01/43.29.73.57
and 01/43.25.82.16

An interesting crowd is found at this restaurant located near the Seine. In good weather, the tables on the small square in front of the restaurant make a great place to dine. Moderate.

La Tour d'Argent
5th/Métro Maubert-Mutualité
15 quai de la Tournelle
Phone: 01/43.54.23.31
Fax: 01/44.07.12.04
Reservations required

Probably the world's most celebrated restaurant. Extraordinary views of the Seine and Notre-Dame. Very Expensive.

Les Bouchons de François Clerc
5th/Métro Maubert-Mutualité
12 rue Hôtel Colbert
Phone: 01/43.54.15.34
Fax: 01/46.34.68.07
Closed Sat. (lunch) and Sun.

Friends who have gone here have loved it (especially the cheese course and reasonably priced wines). Moderate. ❖

sort of thing). There's a lending library upstairs.

Museum of Public Assistance and Hospitals
(Musée de l'Assistance Publique - Hôpitaux de Paris)
5th/Métro Maubert-Mutualité
47 quai de la Tournelle
Closed Mon. and Aug.
Phone: 01/40.27.50.05
Admission: 4€, under 13 free

Interested in exhibits on infanticide or "historic" blood-covered uniforms? Then, this museum will be right up your alley! The 17th-century mansion used to be a pharmacy.

Police Museum
(Musée de la Préfecture de Police)
5th/Métro Maubert-Mutualité
4 rue de la Montagne Ste-Geneviève (2nd floor)
Phone: 01/44.41.52.50
Closed Sun.
Admission: Free

This museum explores the history of the Parisian police force from the 17th century to the present. A must for those interested in guillotines, bombs and Nazi relics. And you don't have to worry about pickpockets as it's located in the police headquarters.

Mosquée de Paris
5th/Métro Monge
2b place du Puits-de-l'Ermite

Phone: 01/45.35.97.33
Closed Fridays and Islamic holidays
Admission: 3€

Modeled after the Alhambra in Spain, this pink mosque was built in the 1920s as a tribute to Muslims from North Africa who supported France in World War I. It's the spiritual center for Muslims in Paris. There's a tea room, a school, and Turkish baths on the premises.

Arènes de Lutèce
5ᵗʰ/Métro Monge
rue Monge and rue de Navarre
Admission: Free

In a word, unique. A first-century Roman arena in the midst of Paris. Not a bad place for a picnic lunch.

Jardin des Plantes
5ᵗʰ/Métro Jussieu or Monge
Off of the Quai St-Bernard, west of Gare d'Austerlitz
Phone: 01/40.79.30.00
Open daily (museums and greenhouses are closed on Tues.)
Admission: To the museum and zoo: 5€. To the greenhouses: 2.50€

Another quiet park in Paris, especially known for its herb garden. The zoo here (the **Ménagerie**) is one of the oldest in the world.

National Museum of Natural History (Musée National d'Histoire Naturelle)
5ᵗʰ/Métro Jussieu

57 rue Cuvier
Phone: 01/40.79.30.00
Closed Tues.
Admission: 7€, 5€ ages 4-16 and over 60, under 4 free

Visit the Gallery of the Evolution of Man and exhibits on everything from entomology (the study of insects) to paleontology (the study of dinosaurs). You're greeted by a huge whale skeleton. You may want to skip the skeletons of fetuses and Siamese twins.

Arab World Institute (Institut du Monde Arabe)
5ᵗʰ/Métro Jussieu
1 rue des Fosses-St-Bernard
Phone: 01/40.51.38.38
Closed Mon.
Admission: Museum: 3€, under 12 free. Exhibits: 7€

This museum of architecture, photography, decorative arts and religion is devoted to providing insight into the Arab world. The modern building in which the museum is housed has striking traditional Arabic geometry etched into the windows.

Jardin Tino Rossi/Musée de la Sculpture en Plein Air
5ᵗʰ/Métro Jussieu
Along quai St-Bernard

A slightly neglected outdoor sculpture garden is found in this park along the Seine near the

Arab World Institute. Don't come here at night.

Musée de Cluny (Musée National du Moyen Age/Thermes de Cluny)
5th/Métro Cluny-La Sorbonne
6 place Paul-Painlevé
Phone: 01/53.73.78.16
Closed Tues.
Admission: 6€, under 18 free

The building that houses this museum (the **Hôtel de Cluny**) has had many lives. It's been a Roman bathhouse in the 3rd century (you can still visit the ruins downstairs), a mansion for a religious abbot in the 15th century, a royal residence, and since 1844, a museum. If you're interested in medieval arts and crafts, you must visit this museum. Chalices, manuscripts, crosses, vestments, carvings, sculptures, and the acclaimed *Lady and the Unicorn* tapestries are all here. You enter through the cobblestoned **Court of Honor (Cour d'Honneur)** surrounded by a Gothic building with gargoyles and turrets. There's also a lovely medieval garden.

place de la Sorbonne
5th/Métro Cluny-La Sorbonne
Off of boulevard St-Michel between the Luxembourg Gardens and boulevard St-Germain-des-Prés

Soak up the college ambience at one of the cafés here in this fountain-filled square. You're near **La Sorbonne**, one of the most famous universities in the world.

Panthéon
5th/Métro Cardinal Lemoine
place du Panthéon
Phone: 01/44.32.18.00
Open daily
Admission: 7€, under 18 free

Originally a church, it's now the burial place for some of the greats of French history, including Voltaire, Victor Hugo, Louis Braille (who created the language for the blind) and Marie Curie (the only woman buried here). Notice the giant frescoes of the life of St. Genevieve.

RESTAURANT TIP
Breakfast in America
5th/Métro Cardinal Lemoin
17 rue des Ecoles
Phone: 01/43.54.50.28
Open daily

Tired of Croissants? If you're homesick for an American breakfast, try the aptly named where you can pretend you're in an American diner and be served eggs, hash browns and coffee (they sometimes even have French toast on the menu). Inexpensive-Moderate. ❖

Paris, are here. Notice the elaborate, carved wood pulpit.

Val-de-Grâce
5th/Métro Gobelins
1 place Alphonse-Laveran
Phone: 01/40.51.51.92
Open afternoons on Tues., Wed. and weekends
Admission: 5€

Once the site of a Benedictine monastery, this huge Baroque building with its famous dome has been a church and a military hospital. Notice all the tiles with the emblem of the *fleur-de-lis*. Anywhere you see this emblem, it means that royalty lived there or went to church there.

St-Etienne-du-Mont
5th/Métro Cardinal Lemoine
1 place Ste-Geneviève
Phone: 01/43.54.11.79
Closed a few hours at lunch and Mon. in summer
Admission: Free

The sight of an ancient abbey (all that's left is the Tower of Clovis), this Gothic church was completed in 1626. The relics of Ste-Geneviève, the patroness of

RESTAURANT TIP
Brasserie Balzar
5th/Métro Odéon
49 rue des Ecoles
Phone: 01/43.54.13.67
Fax: 01/44.07.14.91

This *brasserie* opened in 1898 and serves traditional French cuisine. It's known for its roast chicken, onion soup and "colorful" waiters. Moderate. ❖

∽

6th Arrondissement

Centered around the Boulevard St-Germain, the 6th is filled with upscale galleries, boutiques and restaurants. It's also home to the beautiful and peaceful Luxembourg Gardens.

Institut de France
6th/Métro Pont Neuf (cross the river)
23 quai de Conti
Phone: 01/44.41.44.41
Open daily
Admission: Free (you're only allowed in the courtyard)

You can't miss the grand entrance, towering dome or Baroque décor of this building. It was originally built as a college for students from conquered states. Today, it's the home of five academies to protect French arts, literature and science. One of the academies is the **Académie Français**. It guards the French language. You know, the one that decrees that the French should not use such awful words as "le weekend" or "e-mail."

Museum of Medical History (Musée d'Histoire de la Médecine)
6th/Métro Odéon
12 rue de l'Ecole de Médecine
In the René Descartes University (second floor)
Phone: 01/40.46.16.94

From mid-July to Sept., open afternoons except Thurs. and Sun. The rest of the year, open afternoons except Sat. and Sun. Admission: 3.50€

Yikes! You can see implements used for skull drilling in this 100-year-old museum dedicated to medical history. The implements used to perform Napoleon's autopsy are here, too.

WHAT FLOOR AM I ON?
What we would call the first floor is the *rez-de-chaussée* ("RC" or "0"), the ground floor. The first floor in Paris (*premier étage*) is what we would call the second floor. ❋

Musée de la Monnaie
6th/Métro Odéon
11 quai de Conti
Phone: 01/40.46.55.33
Closed Mon.
Admission: 8€ (includes audio guide), under 16 free

A collection of 30,000 coins and 75,000 medals from Roman times to the euro are found at this museum located in the Paris Mint.

Institut Français d'Architecture
6th/ Métro Odéon
6 bis rue de Tournon
Phone: 01/46.33.90.36
Closed Sun. and Mon.
Admission: Depends on the exhibit

Dedicated to French architects. Exhibits highlight Paris's major architectural events

Luxembourg Gardens (Jardin du Luxembourg)
6th/Métro Cluny-La Sorbonne
a few blocks south of boulevard St-Germain-des-Prés (off of the boulevard St Michel)
Admission: Free

Famous, formal French gardens filled with locals and tourists. Lots of children around the pond playing with wooden sailboats. These gardens are referred to as the heart of the Left Bank. There seem to be birds everywhere. Ernest Hemingway, when he was destitute, is said to have come here to catch pigeons that he then strangled, cooked and ate. Also here is the **Palais du Luxembourg (Luxembourg Palace)**, the home of the French Senate. Tours of the palace by reservation only. The **Musée du Luxembourg** at 19 rue Vaugirard occupies a wing of the Palais du Luxembourg and features temporary exhibitions of some of the big names in the history of art. Open daily. Phone: 01/42.34.25.95. Admission: Depends on the exhibit

St-Sulpice
6th/Métro Mabillon
place St-Sulpice (between the boulevard St-Germain-des-Prés and the Luxembourg Gardens)
Open daily
Admission: Free

Located on an attractive square with a lovely fountain (the

RESTAURANTS TIP

In the **Cour du Commerce** (*6ʰ/Métro Odéon, 61 rue St-André-des-Arts*), you can take a step back in time. A tiny, cobblestone alleyway off of rue St-André-des-Arts that's lined with shops and restaurants, including:

Le Procope
6ʰ/Métro Odéon
13 rue de l'Ancienne Comédie
Phone: 01/40.46.79.00
Fax: 01/40.46.79.09
Open everyday to midnight

Oldest *brasserie* in Paris. Benjamin Franklin is said to have frequented this café. Parisian cuisine at affordable prices served in small dining rooms. Moderate.

Elsewhere in this area, I'd recommend the following:

Chez Maître Paul
6ʰ/Métro Odéon
12 rue Monsieur-le-Prince
Phone: 01/43.54.74.59
Fax: 01/46.34.58.33
Closed Aug.

Hearty cooking of the Jura Mountains and Franche-Comté regions of France (near the Swiss border), known for their game and trout dishes. Moderate.

Polidor
6ʰ/Métro Odéon
41 rue Monsieur-le-Prince
Phone: 01/43.26.95.34

No reservations
No credit cards

Popular 1930s bistro serving inexpensive, traditional Parisian cuisine. Inexpensive.

Roger La Grenouille
6ʰ/Métro Odéon
26 rue des Grands Augustins
Phone: 01/56.24.24.34
Fax: 01/56.24.24.44

This quirky restaurant (it seems that everyone is having fun and the service is friendly) was founded in 1930 and serves good food at moderate prices. Especially good are the *coq au vin* and the *tournedos Rossini*. Moderate.

La Rôtisserie d'en Face
6ʰ/Métro Odéon or St-Michel
2 rue Christine
Phone: 01/43.26.40.98
Fax: 01/43.54.22.71
Closed Sat. (lunch) and Sun.

Modern rotisserie known for its imaginative dishes. Lots of grilled items on the menu. Moderate.

Allard
6ʰ/Métro Odéon
41 rue St-André-des-Arts
Phone: 01/43.26.48.23
Fax: 01/46.33.04.02
Closed Sun. and part of Aug.

Diners repeatedly praise the service and food at this typical Parisian bistro. Moderate.

LUNCH AND A MUSEUM ALL IN ONE

Musée Librairie du Compagnonnage
6th/Métro Mabillon
10 rue Mabillon
Phone: 01/43.26.25.03
Closed Sat. and Sun.
Admission: Free

Once the headquarters for carpenters, this museum and library now displays woodwork throughout history. It's a small museum of only two rooms filled with intricately designed scale models of roofs, steeples and staircases. If you come at lunch, you can eat at **Aux Charpentiers**, a popular Left Bank bistro where the walls are covered with architectural drawings and engravings, and you can have simple bistro fare at reasonable prices. Phone: 01/43.26.30.05.

Fontaine-des-Quatre Points), this church has one of the largest pipe organs in the world with over 6,700 pipes. You'll notice that one of the two bell towers was never completed. Inside are frescoes by Delacroix in the Chapel of the Angels (Chapelle des Anges), a statue of the Virgin and child by Pigalle, and Servandoni's Chapel of the Madonna (Chapelle de la Madone). Set into the floor of the aisle of the north-south transept is a bronze line. On the two equinoxes and the winter solstice, the sun reflects onto a globe and obelisk and from there to a crucifix. The obelisk reads: "Two scientists with God's help."

St-Joseph-des-Carmes
6th/Métro St-Placide
70 rue de Vaugirard
Phone: 01/44.39.52.00
Open daily
Admission: Free

This church was originally a chapel for a Carmelite convent, and was used as a prison during the French Revolution. The crypt contains the remains of 100 priests who were killed in the church's courtyard in 1792 during the Revolution.

Musée Zadkine
6th/Métro Notre-Dame-des-Champs
100 bis rue d'Assas
Phone: 01/55.42.77.20
Closed Mon.
Admission: 4€, under 26 free

SHOPPING TIP

Christian Constant
6th/Métro St-Placide
37 rue d'Assas
Phone: 01/53.63.15.15

Famous shop with chocolates made with ingredients from around the world.

Over 300 pieces of Ossip Zadkine's sculpture (from classic to cubist) are housed in this museum. You can visit the lovely sculpture garden for free.

RESTAURANT TIP
Le Timbre
6ᵗʰ/Métro Notre-Dame-des-Champs
3 rue Ste-Beuve
Closed Sat. (lunch) and Sun.
Phone: 01/45.49.10.40

Good things come in small packages! The name means "stamp," appropriate for this tiny Left Bank bistro. The English chef serves interesting French dishes. Inexpensive-Moderate. ❈

Anatomy Museum
(Musée Orfila)
6ᵗʰ/Métro St-Germain-des-Prés
45 rue des Sts-Pères
(in the René Descartes Université)
Phone: 01/42.86.20.47
Open when the university is open
Admission: Free

Formaldehyde jars with Siamese twins and deformed body parts, wax models of anuses and skinned faces, and the mummified bodies of a whole family are some of the horrid exhibits that greet you in the eighth-floor lobby of this university. Fun!

FAMOUS CAFÉS OF ST-GERMAIN-DES-PRÉS

You have not experienced Paris unless you visit one of its many cafés. Parisians still stop by their local café to meet friends, read the newspaper or just watch the world go by. You should too. It doesn't matter if you order an expensive glass of wine or just a coffee because no one will hurry you. Sitting at a café in Paris is not only a great experience, but also one of the best bargains. If you're watching your euros, you can order and have your drink at the counter. You'll pay less as there's no service charge.

Café Les Deux Magots
6ᵗʰ/Métro St-Germain-des-Prés
6 place St-Germain-des-Prés
Phone: 01/45.48.55.25

If you're a tourist, you'll fit right in at one of Hemingway's favorite spots. I don't really recommend that you eat here (there's a limited menu), but have a drink and enjoy the great people-watching.

Café de Flore
6ᵗʰ/Métro St-Germain-des-Prés
172 boulevard. St-Germain-des-Prés
Phone: 01/45.48.55.26

Another famous café and a favorite of tourists and Parisians alike (next door to Les Deux Magots). At the moment Café de Flore is in fashion with Parisians and Les Deux Magots is not. Why? We're not sure. They look the same to us. ❈

Eglise St-Germain-des-Prés
6th/Métro St-Germain
place St-Germain-des-Prés
Open daily
Admission: Free

This church, located in the fashionable neighborhood that shares its name, dates back to the 6th century. A Gothic choir, 19th-century spire and Romanesque paintings all attest to its long history. It's a frequent and beautiful site for classical concerts.

La Hune
6th/Métro St-Germain-des-Prés
170 boulevard St-Germain
Phone: 01/45.48.35.85

In between Café Les Deux Magots and Café de Flore is this incredible bookstore, packed until midnight with Parisian and foreign "intellectuals." There's an extensive architecture and art section upstairs.

Musée Delacroix
6th/Métro St-Germain-des-Prés
6 rue de Fürstenberg
Phone: 01/44.41.86.50
Closed Tues.
Admission: 4€, under 18 free

Delacroix was one of France's greatest Romantic painters. This museum in Delacroix's former studio and home is off of the small and attractive place Fürstenberg.

place Fürstenberg
6th/Métro St-Germain-des-Prés

Off of the rue l'Abbaye, you'll find a small, quiet square. At its center is a white-globed lamppost. Look familiar? This scenic square has been seen in many films, most recently Martin Scorsese's *The Age of Innocence*. It's often filled with street musicians, some of them surprisingly good.

**FAMOUS MOVIES
FILMED IN PARIS**
2001 *Amélie*
1996 *Everyone Says I Love You*
1994 *Ready to Wear (Prêt-à-Porter)*
1988 *The Accidental Tourist*
1972 *Last Tango in Paris*
1963 *Charade*
1957 *Funny Face*
1951 *An American in Paris*
1943 *Madame Curie*
1925 *Phantom of the Opera*
1923 *Hunchback of Notre Dame*

7th Arrondissement

The chic 7th is home to some of the city's grandest sights, including the Eiffel Tower, Musée d'Orsay and Invalides.

Eiffel Tower (Tour Eiffel)
7th/Métro Trocadéro, Ecole Militaire or Bir-Hakeim
Champ de Mars
Phone: 01/44.11.23.23
Open daily
Admission: To the first landing 4€, second landing 7.30€ and third landing 10.40€. Stairs to the second floor 3.50€
www.tour-eiffel.fr

Constructed for the 1889 Universal Exhibition, the Eiffel Tower was built by the same man who designed the framework for the Statue of Liberty. It was called, among other things, an "iron monster" when it was erected. Gustave-Alexandre Eiffel never meant for his 7,000-ton tower to be permanent and it almost was torn down in 1909. French radio, however, needing a broadcast tower, saved it from destruction. Today, it's without a doubt the most recognizable structure in the world. Well over 200 million people have visited this monument. You can either take the elevator to one of three landings or climb the 1,652 stairs. You cannot visit Paris without a trip to this wonderful structure.

Champ-de-Mars
These long formal gardens (the "Field of Mars") connect the **Eiffel Tower** and the **École Militaire**.

École Militaire
7th/Métro École-Militaire
avenue La Motte-Picquet, Open to the public by special appointment

The Royal Military Academy was built in the mid-1700s to educate the sons of officers of the military. The building is a grand example of the French Classical style with its dome and Corinthian pillars. Its most famous alumnus was Napoleon.

UNESCO Headquarters
7th/Métro Ecole Militaire
7 place de Fontenoy
Closed Sat. and Sun.
Admission: Free

The headquarters of the United Nations Educational, Scientific and Cultural Organization was constructed in 1958 by famous architects from around the world. Lots of glass and concrete and not in a good way. Inside is

8th and 16th Arrondissements

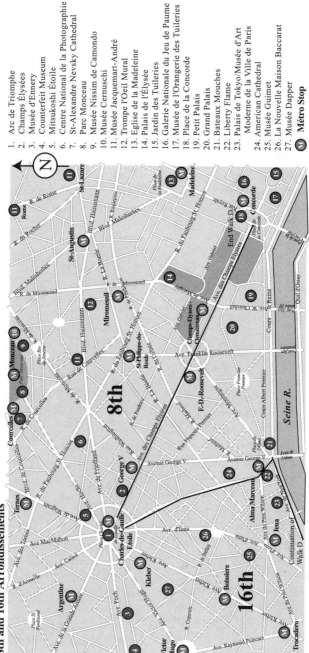

1. Arc de Triomphe
2. Champs Élysées
3. Musée d'Ennery
4. Counterfeit Museum
5. Mitsukoshi Étoile
6. Centre National de la Photographie
7. St-Alexandre Nevsky Cathedral
8. Parc Monceau
9. Musée Nissim de Camondo
10. Musée Cernuschi
11. Musée Jacquemart-André
12. Trompe l'Oeil Mural
13. Eglise de la Madeleine
14. Palais de l'Élysée
15. Jardin des Tuileries
16. Galerie Nationale du Jeu de Paume
17. Musée de l'Orangerie des Tuileries
18. Place de la Concorde
19. Petit Palais
20. Grand Palais
21. Bateaux Mouches
22. Liberty Flame
23. Palais de Tokyo/Musée d'Art Moderne de la Ville de Paris
24. American Cathedral
25. Musée Guimet
26. La Nouvelle Maison Baccarat
27. Musée Dapper
Ⓜ Métro Stop

7th and 15th Arrondissements

1. Eiffel Tower
2. Champ-de-Mars
3. École Militaire
4. UNESCO Headquarters
5. Hôtel des Invalides/ Napoleon's Tomb
6. Army Museum
7. Rodin Museum
8. Assemblée Nationale
9. Basilique Ste-Clotilde
10. Musée d'Orsay
11. Musée Maillol
12. Chapel of Our Lady of the Miraculous Medal
13. Les Egouts (The Sewers)
14. Palais de Chaillot
15. Maison de la Culture du Japon

Métro Stop

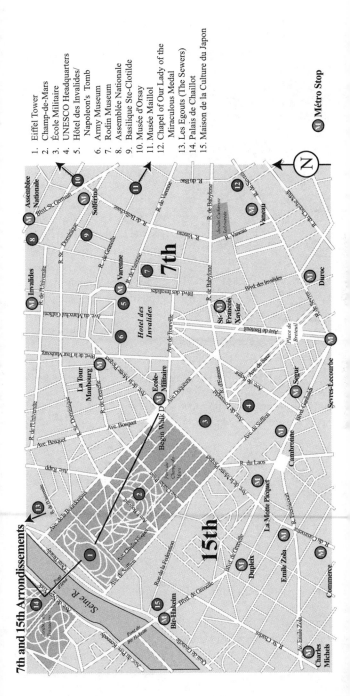

a 20th-century art collection including ceramics by Joan Miró and a giant Picasso mural. Outside is a huge mobile by Calder. The art collection and attractive Japanese garden are free.

Hôtel des Invalides/Army Museum/Napoleon's Tomb
7th/Métro Invalides or La Tour-Maubourg
129 rue de Grenelle
Phone: 01/44.42.38.77
Closed first Mon. of each month
Admission: 7€, under 18 free

Built in 1670 for disabled soldiers, Les Invalides with its golden dome dominates the area around it. The world's greatest military museum, **Musée de l'Armée**, is here (everything from battles of the 1700s through World War II), as is the second tallest monument in Paris, the **Eglise du Dôme** (Dome Church). The main attraction here is **Napoleon's Tomb**, an enormous red stone sarcophagus. For such a tiny man, everything here is huge. Napoleon is best-known for his military feats and the numerous legacies he contributed to France, including the legal code and banking system. Paris owes much of its beauty to the emperor who was responsible for many of the gorgeous monuments still standing in this city. Of course, he had them all built in his honor.

Musée de l'Ordre de la Liberation
7th/Métro Invalides or La Tour-Maubourg
51 bis boulevard de la Tour-Maubourg (enter through the Musée de l'Armée)
Phone: 01/47.05.04.10
Closed on the first Mon. of each month
Admission: 7€, under 18 free

An 18th-century mansion is the home to this museum dedicated to the Resistance and liberation of France. Included are the manuscripts of General de Gaulle and exhibits on the history of the Resistance. Showcases contain uniforms, weapons, clandestine press, transmitters, and relics from the concentration camps. Interesting for history buffs.

RESTAURANT TIP
7ème sud Grenelle
7th/Métro La Tour-Maubourg
159 rue de Grenelle
Phone: 01/44.18.30.30

The odd name means that this restaurant is in the 7th arrondissement at the south end of rue Grenelle. This small modern restaurant serves French, Mediterranean (lots of pasta dishes), and North African (try the *tangine*) cuisine. Friendly service. Moderate. ❧

Rodin Museum (Musée Rodin)
7th/Métro Varenne
77 rue de Varenne
Phone: 01/44.18.61.10
Closed Mon.
Admission: 5€, free under 18. 1€ (garden only)

Rodin is the father of modern sculpture and is known for his sculptures of giant-muscled nudes. This museum is in Rodin's former studio, an 18th-century mansion with a beautiful rose garden. His best-known work, *The Thinker*, is here along with many other major works.

Assemblée Nationale
7th/Métro Invalides
33 quai d'Orsay
Phone: 01.40.63.64.08
Open Apr.-July, Oct.-Nov.
Admission: Free

On the opposite side of the Seine River from the place de la Concorde is the French Parliament. You can visit only from April to July and October to December when Parliament is in session. The grand building, with twelve grand columns supporting a richly carved frieze, was built in the 1700s for the Duchesse of Bourbon. That's why the French call it the Palais Bourbon.

Musée Maillol (Fondation Dina Vierny-Musée Maillol)
7th/Métro Rue du Bac
59-61 rue de Grenelle

Phone: 01/42.22.59.58
Closed. Tues.
Admission: 6€

The museum's permanent collection includes works of Aristide Maillol, a contemporary of Matisse, along with rare sketches by Picasso, Cézanne, Degas and other 20th-century artists. The museum also features revolving exhibits of some of the world's best-known artists. An interesting diversion from all the boutiques in this neighborhood.

SHOPPING TIP
Rue de Grenelle (7th/ Métro Rue du Bac) is home to many fashionable shoe shops. On the same street, check out:

Deyrolle
7th/Métro Rue du Bac
46 rue du Bac
Phone: 01/42.22.30.07
Closed Sun.

This taxidermy shop is "stuffed" with everything from snakes to baby elephants to zebras. Also on display are collections of butterflies, shells, and minerals from all over the world. Kids seem to love this place. Not to be missed, it's so strange, and don't leave without going upstairs.

FOOD ON THE RUN TIP
Barthélemy
7th/Métro Rue du Bac
51 rue de Grenelle
Phone: 01/45.48.56.75
Closed Sun. and Mon.

You can't miss the cream-colored façade of this small but extremely popular cheese shop. This is where Parisians come for their cheese. The staff is extremely knowledgeable and helpful. You'll know when you're getting close because you can smell the shop as you approach. When you walk in, you're overtaken by the intense smell of some of the best cheeses available in France.

Next to the museum at 57-59 rue de Grenelle is the **Fontaine des Quatre-Saisons** (1745). It's decorated with figures representing the four seasons (and a few cherubs thrown in for good measure).

Basilique Ste-Clotilde
7th/Métro Solférino
at rue de Martignac and rue Las Cases
Admission: Free

Completed in 1857, this basilica on a tranquil square has twin Gothic spires. Its huge organ has

56 registers, and is the site of many organ recitals.

SHOPPING TIP

You'll find many antique dealers in the **Carré Rive Gauche** (between St-Germain-des-Prés and the Musée d'Orsay). Take the métro to Rue du Bac and you'll find over 100 antique shops on rue du Bac, rue de Lille and rue de l'Université. ✿

Musée d'Orsay
7ʰ/Métro Solférino
1 rue de la Légion d'Honneur
Phone: 01/40.49.48.14
Closed Mon.
Admission: 7€, under 18 free. 5€ on Sun.

This glass-roofed museum is located across the Seine from the Tuileries and the Louvre in a former train station that has been gloriously converted into 80 galleries. Many of the most famous Impressionist and Post-Impressionist works are here in a building that's a work of art in itself. Some of the paintings here are:

•Whistler's *Whistler's Mother*
•Manet's *Olympia* and *Picnic on the Grass*
•Dega's *Absinthe*
•Renoir's *Moulin de la Galette*

There are also works by Sargent, Pissaro and van Gogh, just to name a few. A magnificent museum, and so much more manageable than the Louvre.

RESTAURANT TIP
Restaurant du Musée d'Orsay
7ʰ/Métro Solférino
1 rue de la Légion d'Honneur
Phone: 01/45.49.47.03
Open for lunch

Located in the beautiful Musée d'Orsay, there's a reasonably priced buffet lunch in an ornate dining room. Not bad for a museum restaurant. Moderate.

Not interested in dining at a museum? Try the roasted chicken at: **Les Deux Musées**, 7ʰ/Métro Solférino, 5 rue Bellechasse, *Phone*: 01/45.55.13.39. Moderate. ✿

Chapel of Our Lady of the Miraculous Medal (Chapelle Notre-Dame de la Médaille Miraculeuse)
7ʰ/Métro Sèvres-Babylone
140 rue du Bac
Open daily
Admission: Free

Catherine Labouré was a young nun when she claimed that the Virgin Mary, dressed in a white silk dress, visited her (four times in 1827) to deliver a design for a holy medal. Go figure! Catherine's body is here in a glass cage. The spot where the Virgin Mary is said to have sat during her visits is a place of veneration. You can buy a rosary or medal in the courtyard (they actually have a machine that dispenses these souvenirs). Another glass cage holds the body of St. Louise de Marillac (one of the founders of the Daughters of Charity). St. Louise is still wearing her habit.

Chapel of the Priests of the Congregation of the Mission
7th/Métro Sèvres-Babylone, 95 rue de Sèvres

*Open daily
Admission: Free*

Around the corner from the previous chapel the waxed corpse of St. Vincent de Paul (known for his charity) is found in an ornate glass and silver casket above the main altar. If you like this sort of macabre stuff, you can climb the stairs and get a close-up view of his body.

The Sewers (Les Egouts)
*7th/Métro Alma-Marceau
Pont de l'Alma (opposite 93 quai d'Orsay)
Phone: 01/53.68.27.81
Closed Thurs., Fri. and part of Jan.
Admission: 4€, under 5 free*

Why would you want to visit the sewers of Paris? Many do, despite the smell (especially bad in summer). You can visit the huge underground passages in the bowels of the city (no pun intended), a museum, and view a film.

8th Arrondissement

Luxurious shopping, the place de la Concorde, the Champs-Élysées and the Arc de Triomphe are all found in the 8th.

Arc de Triomphe
8th/Métro Charles-de-Gaulle-Étoile
place Charles-de-Gaulle-Étoile
Phone: 01/55.37.73.77
Open daily.
Admission: 7€, under 18 free

Don't try to walk across the square. This is Paris's busiest intersection. Twelve streets pour into the circle around the Arc. There are underground passages that will take you to the Arc. It's the largest triumphal arch in the world. Napoleon commissioned it in 1806 and it was completed in 1836. The Arc is the home to the Tomb of the Unknown Soldier, and is engraved with the names of generals in Napoleon's victories.

One of the most famous images of the Arc de Triomphe occurred on June 14, 1940, when the Nazi army marched under the Arc. Newsreel cameras captured the French openly weeping. A happier sight occurs today when, each April, runners sprint down the Champs-Élysées in the **International Marathon of Paris**.

There's an observation deck providing one of the greatest views of Paris. There's no cost to visit the Arc, but there's an admission fee for the exhibit of photos of the Arc throughout history and for the observation deck. If you aren't impressed by the view down the Champs-Élysées, you really shouldn't have come to Paris.

Mitsukoshi Étoile
8th/Métro Charles-de-Gaulle-Étoile
3 rue de Tilsitt
Phone: 01/44.09.11.11
Closed Sun. and Mon.
Admission: 3€

On the site of a famous kimono boutique, this museum cel-

SHOPPING TIP
Publicis Drugstore
8th/Métro Champs-Élysées
133 bis Avenue des Champs-Élysées
Phone: 01/44.43.77.64

Opened in 1958 and recently renovated, this is not just a drugstore on a famous street. You'll also find boutiques, a newsstand, wine shop, specialty-food market and a casual restaurant. ❧

ebrates cultural exchange between France and Japan, not to mention a section dedicated to the history of the kimono.

Avenue des Champs-Élysées
8th/Métro Champs- Élysées
At the east end is place de la Concorde and on the west is the Arc de Triomphe.

One of the most famous streets in the world. It's been the site of the somber yet impressive victory parade of the Allies in World War II, the annual military parade every July 14, and the final leg of the Tour de France bicycle race. The Champs-Élysées is home to expensive retail shops, fast-food chains, car dealers, banks, huge movie theatres and overpriced cafés. Despite this, you can sit at a café and experience great people-watching (mostly tourists, but one of the most diverse groups of people you'll ever see).

ENTERTAINMENT TIP
Le Lido
8th/Métro Champs-Élysées
116 bis Avenue des Champs-Élysées
Phone: 01/40.76.56.10
Admission: 60-80€, 140-200€
(with dinner)

Elaborate costumes, special effects, sixty Bluebell Girls and the Lido Boy dancers and even ice skating make for an interesting evening at this famous cabaret. It's not for everyone, but people have been enjoying the show since 1946. ❧

SHOPPING TIPS
Just around the corner from the Champs-Élysées at 40 rue Marbeuf is **Élysées Stylos Marbeuf**, *Phone: 01/42.25.40.49*, Closed Sun. This wonderful little shop with a knowledgeable and pleasant staff will help you pick out just the right pen. The French love their pens, and at this shop you can bring home a souvenir pen, desk accessory or leather goods.

One interesting shop on the Champs-Élysées is the large **Sephora Perfume Store** at 74 Champs-Élysées (open daily until midnight). The large "wheel of scents" lets you smell scents from chocolate to flower to wood! ❧

Pavillon Elysée
8th/Métro Champs-Élysées
10 avenue Champs-Élysées
Phone: 01/42.65.85.10

The Pavillon Élysées is an elegant oblong glass building built for the 1900 World's Fair. For decades, a string of different restaurants and cafés set up shop here. It's been fixed up by **Lenôtre**. Gaston Lenôtre opened his first pastry shop in 1947. Today, Lenôtre has eight shops throughout Paris. Right on the Champs-Élysées, you'll find a café, kitchen shop and cooking school all in one. Lenôtre's specialty is its desserts. Have one with a cup of delicious coffee on the lovely stone terrace that looks onto the gardens. Then, head inside to Le Comptoir, the cooking shop where you can buy everything from cooking utensils to bottles of wine. You can sign up for cooking classes taught by chefs from throughout the French-speaking world. Some classes are held in English. These cooking workshops cost 105€. A shrine to food in the heart of Paris.

Grand Palais
8th/Métro Champs-Élysées
avenue Winston-Churchill off of
the Champs-Élysées
Phone: 01/44.13.17.30
Closed Tues.
Admission: Depends on the exhibit

Built for the 1900 World Exhibition (along with the Eiffel Tower), this magnificent glass and metal palace has been recently renovated. Just like the Eiffel Tower, it was never meant to be a permanent structure, but remains today in all its glory, and has been returned to its previous purpose as host to premier exhibits. On the other side of avenue Winston-Churchill is the equally beautiful but smaller and appropriately named **Petit Palais**, where the city's large art collection is housed.

Palais de l'Élysée
8th/Métro Champs-Élysées
55 rue Faubourg St-Honoré
Closed to the public

The "Élysée," as the French call it, has been the elegant home of the French president since 1873. Built in 1718, it has had many lives. During the revolution, it served as a print shop. You can only gaze through the gate as it's closed to the public. That's why all those guards are outside.

Marché aux Timbres
8th/Métro Champs-Élysées or
Franklin-D.-Roosevelt
off of the Champs-Élysées at Rond-Point/near the junction of avenues
Gabriel and Marigny
Open 10 a.m. to 5 p.m. on Thursdays, weekends and holidays

Stamps from all over the world and vintage postcards can be found at the stamp market off the Champs-Élysées at Rond-Point. Made famous in the 1963 movie *Charade* featuring Audrey Hepburn and Cary Grant, which was filmed almost entirely in Paris.

place de la Concorde
8th/Métro Concorde
Between the Jardin Des Tuileries and the Champs-Élysées

This square is huge (21 acres) and in the center stands the **Obelisk of Luxor**, an Egyptian column from the 13th century covered with hieroglyphics. It was moved here in 1833. Now a traffic roundabout, it was here that King Louis XVI and Marie Antoinette were guillotined during the French Revolution. The name is ironic as *concorde* means "harmony."

Métro Concorde
At the place de la Concorde

The Concorde métro stop has 44,000 blue-and-white lettered ceramic tiles on its walls. They spell out the seventeen articles of the declaration of the *Rights of Man and the Citizens* that the National Assembly adopted in 1789.

Too much history? Too many sights? Check out the lobby of one of the luxury hotels near the place de la Concorde. Oh, you aren't a guest? Just act like you belong and you'll likely not get stopped. If you're afraid to visit the hotels, enjoy an elegant tea at the fashionable and fancy Bernardaud, 8 bis Galerie Royale (11 rue Royale).

Where to have a refreshing drink after a walk in the area surrounding the Champs-Élysées? Try the **Buddha Bar**, 8 rue Boissy d'Anglas. See and be seen at this trendy Asian-themed bar.

Rue du Faubourg-St-Honoré

In the 1700s, this street was home to the richest residents of Paris. Today, it's home (along with nearby **avenue Montaigne**) to designer boutiques. Window-shopping for the wealthy.

If you're tired of Dior, Saint Laurent and other boutiques on rue du Faubourg-St-Honoré, try these wonderful non-clothing boutiques:

•**Les Caves Taillevent**
8th/Métro Charles-de-Gaulle-Étoile or St-Philippe-du-Roule
199 rue du Faubourg-St-Honoré
Phone: 01/45.61.14.09

This wine shop is associated with the well-known Taillevent restaurant, and is said to have over 500,000 bottles of wine starting at around 5€.

•**Mariage-Frères**
8th/Métro Ternes
260 rue du Faubourg St-Honoré
Phone: 01/46.22.18.54

Four hundred types of tea offered in elegant salons serving light meals (with no-smoking sections).

•**La Maison du Chocolat**
8th/Métro Ternes
225 rue du Faubourg-St-Honoré
Phone: 01/42.27.39.44
Closed Sun.

Every chocolate lover should visit this place.

St-Alexandre Nevsky Cathedral

8th/Métro Ternes
12 rue Daru
Open times vary
Admission: Free

A Russian Orthodox cathedral, complete with onion-shaped domes. It's filled with rich icons and mosaics.

RECREATION TIP

For a break from hectic Paris, stop in the beautiful **Parc Monceau** surrounded by 18th- and 19th-century mansions (a few blocks northeast from the Arc de Triomphe down avenue Hoche and avenue Van Dyck). ❊

Musée Nissim de Camondo

8th/Métro Monceau
63 rue de Monceau
Phone: 01/53.89.06.50
Closed Mon. and Tues.
Admission: 6€, under 18 free

This museum is dedicated to 18th-century *objets d'art* and furniture. Located in a mansion overlooking the beautiful Parc Monceau, it showcases objects owned by such notables as Marie Antoinette. The kitchen of the mansion has been painstakingly restored.

Chinese Pagoda
8th/Métro Courcelles
48 rue de Courcelles (about a block from Parc Monceau)

What is a bright-red Chinese pagoda doing in the middle of all these fancy mansions? Monsieur Loo was a successful Asian antiques dealer. In 1922, he had a French mansion converted into a traditional Chinese house–a pagoda–complete with a dragon and lion motif and a gate decorated with guard lions.

Musée Cernuschi
8th/Métro Monceau
7 avenue Vélasquez
Phone: 01/45.63.50.75
Closed Mon.
Admission: Free

Cernuschi was a banker from Milan who bequeathed his beautiful home and incredible collection of Asian art to the city. A must for Asian-art aficionados. There's also a collection of Persian bronze objects.

Eglise de la Madeleine
8th/Métro Madeleine
place de la Madeleine
Open daily
Admission: Free

This neo-Classical church has 52 Corinthian columns and provides a great view (from the top of the monumental steps) of the place de la Concorde. Huge bronze doors depicting the Ten Commandments provide the impressive entry to the marble and light-filled interior. There are three giant domes and a huge pipe organ. The painting in the chancel depicts the history of Christianity. Such grand events as the funerals of Chopin and Coco Chanel (now there's a pair!) were held here.

On the east side of the church is a beautiful **flower market**. Underground are Paris's most interesting **public toilets**. Dating back to 1905, these Art Nouveau "masterpieces" have elaborate tiles, stained glass (in every stall) and beautiful carved woodwork. There's an elaborate "throne" for shoe shining. Go even if you don't have to "go." By the way, did you know that the female bathroom attendants are known as "Madames Pipis?"

The area around the place de la Madeleine (8th/Métro Madeleine) is packed with fabulous specialty food shops (the windows of the food store Fauchon are worth a trip by themselves), wine dealers, restaurants, and tea rooms. This is a perfect place for eating and purchasing culinary souvenirs. There's something for every taste but this is an upscale area, and can be expensive. Begin at Lavinia and continue around the place:

•Lavinia
3-5 boulevard de la Madeleine
Phone: 01/42.97.20.20
Closed Sun. Open until 8:00 p.m.

The largest wine shop in Paris with 2,000 foreign wines, 3,000 French wines and 1,000 spirits, priced from 3 to 3,600 euros. Drink any bottle from the shop at the wine bar. Lunch served—with wine, of course. No dinner.

•Boutique Maille
6 place de la Madeleine
Phone: 01/40.15.06.00
Closed Sun.

Boutique mustard shop.

•L'Ecluse
15 place de la Madeleine
Phone: 01/48.05.19.12

Chain of trendy wine bars. Not the greatest food in Paris, but great for wine tasting (especially Bordeaux).

•Caviar Kaspia
17 place de la Madeleine
Phone: 01/42.65.33.32 (restaurant)/01/42.65.66.21 (store)
Closed Sun.

Caviar, blinis and salmon. There's also a restaurant upstairs.

•Hédiard
21 place de la Madeleine
Phone: 01/43.12.88.88
Closed Sun.

Food store/spice shop that's been open since the 1850s, similar to Fauchon, with an on-site restaurant. (*Phone*: 01/43.12.88.99).

•Nicolas
31 place de la Madeleine
Phone: 01/44.51.90.22
Closed Sun.

Located upstairs from the Nicolas wine shop. You can buy a bottle of wine at the shop and have it served with your meal. The menu is limited, but the wines sold by the glass are inexpensive.

•Fauchon
26 place de la Madeleine
Phone: 01/47.42.60.11
Closed Sun.

Deli and grocery known for its huge selection of canned food, baked goods and alcohol. The store is a must for those wanting to bring back French specialties.

•La Maison du Miel
24 rue Vignon
Phone: 01/47.42.26.70
Closed Sun.

This food store contains everything made from honey (from sweets to soap), and is located around the corner from Fauchon.

•Marquise de Sévigné
32 place de la Madeleine
Phone: 01/42.65.19.47

A French "luxury" (their word) chocolate maker since 1898.

Near the place de la Madeleine are:

•Ladurée
16 rue Royale
Phone: 01/42.60.21.79

Expensive and elegant *salon de thé* and pastry shop.

•Albert Ménès
41 boulevard Malesherbes
Phone: 01/42.66.95.63
Closed Sun. and mid-July to mid-Aug.

Gourmet food shop that specializes in items from the provinces.

Les Caves Augé
8th/Métro St-Augustin
116 boulevard Haussmann
Phone: 01/45.22.16.97

Famous wine shop since 1850.

And now back to the sights!

Trompe l'Oeil Mural
8th/Métro Miromesnil
at the corner of rue de Penthievre and avenue Delcassé

This ingenious mural features a man looking from his balcony at a nude while doves fly away from him. An incredible example of "fooling the eye."

Musée Jacquemart-André
8th/Métro Miromesnil
158 boulevard Haussmann
Phone: 01/45.62.11.59
Open daily
Admission: 9€, under 7 free

Among the department stores and shops on boulevard Haussmann is this museum featuring art, especially from the Italian Renaissance. Jacquemart and André collected rare paintings and decorative art in this 1850s mansion. Although the museum with its paintings by Rembrandt, Bellini, Carpaccio, Van Dyck and Rubens is memorable, the opulent mansion is the real star here. Marble staircases, chandeliers and elaborately painted ceilings seem to hold your attention rather than the paintings on the walls. The high-ceilinged dining room, with its 18th-century tapestries, is a popular place to rest and have tea, a salad or pastry.

Centre National
de la Photographie
8th/Métro George-V
11 rue Berryer
Phone: 01/53.76.12.31
Closed Tues.
Admission: 5€

Exhibits feature photography from France and throughout the world.

American Cathedral of the Holy Trinity
8ᵗʰ/Métro Alma-Marceau or Georges-V
23 avenue George V
Phone: 01/53.23.84.00
Open daily
Admission: Free

One of Europe's best examples of Gothic Revival architecture, this cathedral is a little bit of the United States in Paris. Kneelers are done in needlepoint featuring the fifty state flowers. Frequent choral concerts are held here. The cloister commemorates Americans who died in Europe during the world wars. Church services are held in English. It's also the only air-conditioned church in Paris. How American!

Pont de l'Alma/place de l'Alma
Border of 8ᵗʰ and 16ᵗʰ/Métro Alma-Marceau

The area around the place de l'Alma is one of the most luxurious in Paris. The square (**place de l'Alma**) and the bridge (**Pont de l'Alma**) were created in the time of Napoleon III. The original bridge was replaced in 1972 with the present-day steel structure. Take a look at one of the fanciest high-water markers in the world. Originally, there were four Second Empire soldier statues that decorated the old bridge.

AN ENGLISH PUB IN PARIS
The Cricketer
8ᵗʰ/Métro St-Augustin
41 rue des Mathurins
Phone: 01/40.07.01.45

British brew, pub food and walls covered with cricket memorabilia. Yes, they do speak English here. ❧

Only one, Zouave, remains below the bridge. Parisians use it to measure the height of the water in the Seine. It's said that in 1910, the water reached all the way to Zouave's chin.

Bateaux-Mouches
If you're visiting Paris for the first time, a good way to tour the Seine and get a good overview of Paris is on the Bateaux-Mouches boat tour. The boats depart regularly from the Right Bank next to the place de l'Alma. (Métro Alma-Marceau). You have your choice of a 75-minute day cruise (for about 7€) or lunch and dinner cruises.

Liberty Flame/Shrine to Princess Diana
Border of 8ᵗʰ and 16ᵗʰ/Métro Alma-Marceau, on place de l'Alma at the north end (Right Bank) of Pont de l'Alma
Admission: Free

A replica of the torch of the Statue of Liberty was erected here in 1987. It was meant to commemorate the French Resistance during World War II. It just happens to be over the tunnel where Princess Diana and her boyfriend Dodi Al-Fayedh were killed in an automobile crash in 1997. The Liberty Flame is now an unofficial shrine covered with notes, flowers and prayers to the dead princess.

Avenue Montaigne
8th/Métro Alma-Marceau

This avenue was once known as allée des Veuves (Widows' Alley) and was the sight of the infamous Mabille Dance Hall until 1870. Today, it's lined with elegant buildings. You'll find art galleries, banks, and some of the most famous luxury boutiques here. If you're looking for major fashion designers and luxury shops such as Christian Dior, Lacroix, Cartier and Versace, you've come to the right avenue.

~

16th Arrondissement

Along with the 8th, you'll find upscale shopping, luxurious residences and parks such as the Trocadéro.

> **LOCATING AN ADDRESS**
> Address numbers begin at the river for north-south streets. East-west addresses run parallel to the Seine River (following the course of the river). Street signs aren't like at home. They are at the corner of the street, but usually on a plaque attached to the building, way above eye level. ❧

Fondation Mona Bismarck
16th/Métro Alma-Marceau
34 avenue de New-York
Phone: 01/47.23.38.88
Closed. Sun. and Mon.
Admission: Free

This foundation presents exhibits aimed to introduce American culture to France. Always interesting and the exhibits are graciously presented.

Palais de Chaillot
16th/Métro Trocadéro
place du Trocadéro

Across the river from the Eiffel Tower is the Trocadéro neighborhood. The **Trocadéro Gardens (Jardins du Trocadéro)** are home to the large **Palais de Chaillot**. This huge palace, surrounded by more than 60 fountains, was built 60 years ago and is home to several museums (**Musée de la Marine**, a naval museum; **Musée du Patrimoine et l'Architecture**, housing reproductions of famous monuments; and **Musée de l'Homme**, an anthropology museum). Admission to the museums is 7€ and they are closed on Tuesday.

What would Paris be without a glass of French champagne? One very elegant and expensive place to drink bubbly is: **Trocadéro Dokhans Hôtel**, 16ᵗʰ/Métro Trocadéro, 117 rue Lauriston, Phone: 01/53.65.66.99, open daily (evenings only). An elegant champagne bar where you can enjoy it by the flute or by the bottle.

Cimetière du Passy
16ᵗʰ/Métro Trocadéro
2 rue Comandant-Schloesing
Phone: 01/47.27.51.42
Open daily
Admission: Free

This small cemetery filled with chestnut trees is behind the Palais de Chaillot. Among the famous buried here are composer Debussy and painter Manet.

Musée d'Art Moderne de la Ville de Paris/Musée des Enfants
16ᵗʰ/Métro Iéna
11 avenue du Président Wilson
Phone: 01/53.67.40.00
Closed Mon.
Admission: Permanent collection is free

This museum houses the city's modern art collection (including murals by Matisse), and hosts traveling exhibits. The connected museum hosts exhibits for children. Most exhibits here don't have English translations.

Palais de Tokyo
16ᵗʰ/Métro Iéna
13 avenue du Président Wilson
Phone: 01/47.23.54.01
Closed Mon.
Admission: 5€

This colossal Art Nouveau building is a contemporary art center. Its courtyard is a popular, even if unlikely, spot for skateboarders.

Musée National des Arts Asiatiques
16ᵗʰ/Métro Iéna
6 place d'Iéna
Phone: 01/56.52.53.00
Closed. Tues.
Admission: 7€, under 18 free

Also known as the **Musée Guimet**, this museum houses a world-famous collection of Asian art.

Musée Galliera – Musée de la Mode de la Ville de Paris
16th/Métro Iéna
10 avenue Pierre-1er-de-Serbie
Phone: 01/56.52.86.00
Closed Mon.
Admission: 7€, under 14 free

This museum showcases the history of gowns and accessories of *haute couture* in a 19th century palace.

La Nouvelle Maison Baccarat
16th/Métro Boissiere
11 place des Etats-Unis
Phone: 01/40.22.11.00
Closed Sun.
Admission: 7€

Crystal museum and boutique operated by the crystal company of the same name. The setting is appropriate, a 1900 stone mansion, with dozens of crystal chandeliers (all for sale for over $100,000, in case you're interested). Across the street is the **Cristal Room Baccarat** restaurant.

Musée Marmottan-Claude Monet
16th/Métro La Muette
2 rue Louis-Boilly
Phone: 01/42.24.07.02
Closed Mon.
Admission: 7€, under 8 free

Monet fans can take in his paintings, including *Impression-Sunrise* from which the Impressionist movement is said to have gotten its name. In addition to the well-known water lillies and paintings of his house in Giverny, you'll also see Renoir's portrait of Monet. The museum is named after Paul Marmottan who donated his beautiful home to house his collection of historic furnishings (also on display here). In 1966, when Monet's son died in an automobile accident, this museum received over 130 works of Claude Monet.

Wine Museum (Musée du Vin)
16th/Métro Passy
5 square Charles Dickens off of the rue des Eaux
Phone: 01/45.25.63.26
Closed Mon.
Admission: 8€

The Wine Museum is dedicated to France's winemaking heritage. Exhibits of tools and memorabilia allow you to discover its ancient traditions. It's located in ancient vaults and cellars dating back to the Middle Ages. Oh, and admission includes one glass of wine!

Maison de Balzac
16th/Métro Passy
47 rue Raynouard
Phone: 01/55.74.41.80
Closed Mon.
Admission: Free

Honoré de Balzac was one of the great French writers. He is most well known for his *La Comédie Humaine*–a collection of stories, many of which are set in Paris. His home and garden are popular with the French. Rodin's bust of Balzac is here.

Musée Dapper
16th/Métro Victor-Hugo
35 bis rue Paul-Valéry
Phone: 01/45.00.01.50
Closed Mon. and Tues.
Admission: 5€

This museum is dedicated to the culture and art of Africa. Interesting exhibits, but many are not in English. It's a meeting place for Africans living in Paris.

Musée National du Sport
16th/Métro Porte de St-Cloud
24 rue du Commandant Guilbaud
Phone: 01/40.45.99.12
Closed Sat.
Admission: 5€

This museum is located in the **Parc des Princes** stadium (at the main entrance), and its exhibits look at the last 150 years of sports and their popularity in modern society.

Tenniseum Roland-Garros
16th/Métro Porte d'Auteuil
Phone: 01/47.43.48.48
2 ave. Gordon-Bennett
Admission: 8€

Until recently, access to the Roland-Garros Stadium has been limited to spectators coming to see the French Open. The stadium is now open year-round with guided tours (some in English). A multimedia museum ("Tenniseum") is devoted to 500 years of tennis history. Visitors can watch 200 hours of tennis action, visit a huge library devoted solely to tennis, and kids can participate in workshops with their parents. A must for tennis lovers.

Counterfeit Museum
(Musée de la Contrefaçon)
16th/Métro Porte Dauphine
16 rue de la Faisanderie
Phone: 01/56.26.14.00
Open Tues.-Sun. afternoons.
Closed Mon. and weekends in Aug.
Admission: 2.50€

Everything fake (next to the authentic item) at this strange museum. Housed in a beautiful mansion (its been featured in many commercials), you'll see counterfeit money, cigars and even "Rodin" bronze sculptures.

Musée d'Ennery
16th/Métro Porte Dauphine
59 avenue Foch
Phone: 01/45.53.57.96
Currently closed for renovation
Admission: Free

Seven thousand pieces of Asian ornaments, furniture and ceramics are on display at this museum.

Scheduled to reopen after years of renovation.

Bois de Boulogne
on the western edge of the 16th/ Métro Porte Dauphine

An enormous park (nearly 2,200 acres) open 24 hours a day (avoid it at night). Walking paths, lakes, a waterfall, an amusement park (see below), children's zoo and two horse racetracks are all here. **Parc de St-Cloud** is another less crowded park at the western end of métro line 10 (Métro Boulogne/Pont de St-Cloud). Come here for fountains, flowers, ponds and tranquil walks.

Jardin d'Acclimatation
16th/Métro Porte Maillot
Phone: 01/40.67.90.82

Open daily
Admission: 3€, under 3 free

The northern 25 acres of the **Bois de Boulogne** is just the place for kids. On Wednesdays, Saturdays and Sundays take a ride on the yellow and green train to the amusement-park entrance from the Porte Maillot métro stop, which departs every 30 minutes. Playgrounds, pony rides, a zoo, miniature golf course, bowling alleys, a hall of mirrors …you get the picture. La Prévention Routière is probably the most interesting attraction. It's a miniature roadway where children drive small cars. Real police officers (*gendarmes*) teach kids to follow and obey stoplights and street signs

❧

9th Arrondissement

The 9th is home to the opulent Opéra Garnier, and a center for shopping (most major department stores are here) and nightlife.

Department Stores on Boulevard Haussmann
Boulevard Haussmann is the home to the top two department stores in Paris. **Galeries Lafayette** at 40 blvd. Haussmann (9th/

Métro Chaussée d'Antin) opened in 1894. You'll find designer clothes, a wonderful food hall and a free view of Paris from the 7th floor. **Au Printemps** at 64 blvd. Haussmann (9th/Métro Havre-Caumartin) opened in 1864. Here, you'll find designer clothing, household goods and furniture. The tea room on the 6th floor has a stained-glass ceiling. Which is better? You decide.

THE MOST IMPORTANT
PARISIAN YOU'VE NEVER
HEARD OF

The most important Parisian you may never have heard of is **Baron George-Eugene Haussmann**. Haussmann was appointed by Napoleon III to give Paris a facelift. He cleared slums, improved the sewer and water systems, developed parks, and created Paris's grand avenues. His work is largely responsible for the fantastic Paris we see today. ❧

Opéra Garnier
9ᵗʰ/Métro Opéra
place de l'Opéra
Phone: 01/40.01.22.63
Open daily.
Admission: 6€

Built in 1875, this ornate opera house now is the showplace for both opera and dance. It's often referred to as the most opulent theater in the world. Chandeliers, marble stairways, red-velvet boxes, a ceiling painted by Chagall, and a facade of marble and sculpture all make this the perfect place for an elegant night out in Paris. The box office telephone number is 08/92.69.78.68. There's also a museum celebrating opera and dance over the years. Closed Sun.

Musée de la
Parfumerie-Fragonard
9ᵗʰ/Métro Opéra
9 rue Scribe
Phone: 01/47.42.04.56
Closed Sun.
Admission: Free

Located in a lovely 1860 town house, this museum is devoted to the history of perfume from the time of the Egyptians to today.

Paris-Story
9ᵗʰ/Métro Opéra
11 bis rue Scribe
Phone: 01/42.66.62.06
Open daily. Show hourly.
Admission: 8€, 5€ under 18

Okay, so it's really touristy. This 45-minute multimedia show is a good introduction to what Paris has to offer and is an interesting

RESTAURANT TIP
Café de la Paix
9ᵗʰ/Métro Opéra
12 boulevard des Capucines
(place de l'Opéra)
Phone: 01/40.07.30.20

Famous café (not really known for its food). Popular with tourists. Another spot for outdoor people-watching (and the inside is beautiful). Moderate-Expensive. ❧

educational experience (especially for children) as it highlights the history of Paris. Headphones provide translations in 12 languages.

Grévin Wax Museum
9th/Métro Grands Boulevards
10 boulevard Montmartre
Phone: 01/47.70.85.05.
Open daily
Admission: 16€, 9€ ages 6-14, under 6 free

This wax museum dates back to the late 1800s, and is a 3-D showcase for figures from French history as well as modern celebrities (all in wax, of course). Strange, but certainly a different Parisian experience.

Drouot-Richelieu Auctions
9th/Métro Richelieu-Drouot
9 Rue Drouot
Phone: 01/48.00.20.20
Closed Sun.
Admission: Free

This huge auction house has stood on the corner of rues Drouot and Rossini since the mid-1800s. An "exposition" of items for sale is held the day before and from 11:00 a.m. to noon the morning of the auction. You can inspect everything from paintings and furniture to wine and ancient objects in the auction house's sixteen rooms. A truly interesting experience and, if the price is right, you may come home with a little bit of Paris.

Grande Synagogue de la Victoire
9ᵗʰ/Métro Peletier
44 rue de la Victoire
Not open to the public

This is the second-largest synagogue in Europe. You'll only be able to admire its facade (representing the Tablets) as, unfortunately, it's closed to the public.

> **RESTAURANT TIP**
> **Au Petit Riche**
> *9ᵗʰ/Métro Le Peletier*
> *25 rue Le Peletier (at rue Rossini)*
> *Phone: 01/47.70.68.68*
> *Fax: 01/48.24.10.79*
> *Closed Sun.*
>
> This bistro serves specialties of the Loire Valley with a Parisian twist. Try the *civet* (game stew). Moderate. ❖

Musée Gustave-Moreau
9ᵗʰ/Métro Trinité
14 rue de la Rochefoucauld
Phone: 01/48.74.38.50
Closed Tues.
Admission: 4€, under 18 free

Gustave Moreau was a mentor to Matisse. He designed and established this museum before his death in 1898. His residence and studio have been converted to a museum honoring him, and you'll find paintings by others (such as Rembrandt) thrown into the mix.

> **RESTAURAUNT TIP**
> **Bistro de Deux Théâtres**
> *9ᵗʰ/Métro Blanche or Trinité*
> *18 rue Blanche*
> *Phone: 01/45.26.41.43*
> *Fax: 01/48.74.08.92*
>
> Affordable dining at this neighborhood bistro near the place de Clichy. Moderate. ❖

Musée de la Vie Romantique
9ᵗʰ/Métro Blanche
16 rue Chaptal
Phone: 01/55.31.95.67
Closed Mon.
Admission: Permanent collection is free

Housed in an Italianate villa, the first floor showcases the personal effects of novelist George Sand, including her watercolors. The second floor is devoted to the collection of painter Ary Scheffer of the Romantic movement (from which the museum takes its name). The museum is lovely, especially the garden and greenhouse.

10th Arrondissement

The 10th is home to two great train stations, the Gare du Nord and Gare de l'Est. It wasn't too long ago that guidebooks didn't even mention the 10th (other than perhaps a trip to Brasserie Flo). Today, this working-class area is increasingly popular with artists, making for an interesting mix. Boutiques, cafés, galleries and trendy restaurants seem to have multiplied overnight.

Gare du Nord
10th/Métro Gare du Nord
rue de Dunkerque

The grandest of all 19th-century train stations. It's taken on added importance since 1994 when it became the Eurostar terminal (the train that runs through the "Chunnel" between London and Paris).

Canal St-Martin
Between the place de la République and the Parc de la Villette

Winding through the 10th arrondissement on Paris's northeast side is the beautiful **Canal St.-Martin**. The canal's bridges, footbridges and locks have been renovated. It's a great place to walk, or, if a scenic canal tour is more to your liking, boats depart from the quai de la Loire (19th/Métro Jaurès).

LONDON MADE EASY
Should you dine in London? It's possible. While I can't imagine why you'd want to leave Paris, you could be in London in a mere three hours. The Eurostar train speeds you through the French and English countryside and through the Channel Tunnel (the "Chunnel"), allowing you to visit Paris and London in the same day.

You leave Paris's Gare du Nord station and arrive in London's Waterloo station. Fares are 200€ (one-way), 300€ (round-trip second-class), 280€ (one-way first-class) and 440€ (round-trip first-class). Reservations can be made by contacting Eurostar at 800/EUROSTAR or www.raileurope.com.

For more information on visiting London, pick up Open Road's *London Made Easy*. ❀

Eglise St-Vincent de Paul
10th/Métro Gare du Nord
place Franz-Liszt
Phone: 01/48.78.47.47
Open daily
Admission: Free

Sitting on top of terraced gardens, this church dates back to the mid-1800s. It has a columned portico and twin towers, and inside, there are beautiful frescoes.

Pinacothèque de Paris
10ᵗʰ/Métro Bonne-Nouvelle
30 bis rue de Paradis
Phone: 01/43.25.71.41
Open daily
Admission: Depends on the exhibit

The goal of this for-profit museum is to present expositions of rare, private art collections. Its first exhibit was the private Picasso collection owned by his last wife. In the future, there will be a permanent collection on display. It's an interesting idea in a city of many museums, some charging small admission or no admission at all. The intention is to create an international network of museums and to rotate major exhibitions.

> **SHOPPING TIP**
> Into crystal and porcelain? **Rue de Paradis** (10th/ Métro Gare de l'Est) is the street to walk down. ❖

> **ENTERTAINMENT TIP**
> New Morning
> *10ᵗʰ/Métro Château d'Eau*
> *7 rue des Petites-Ecuries*
> *Phone: 01/45.23.51.41*
>
> This spartan music club (in the increasingly trendy 10ᵗʰ) is where you come to hear jazz, world music and folk. ❖

Passage Brady
10ᵗʰ/ Métro Château d'Eau

You can enter this narrow *passage* around 33 boulevard Strasbourg and find mostly Indian, but also Turkish and Moroccan, restaurants in a strangely exotic setting. These are inexpensive restaurants in a working-class neighborhood.

> **RESTAURANT TIP**
> Brasserie Flo
> *10ᵗʰ/Métro Château d'Eau*
> *7 cour des Petites-Écuries (enter from 63 rue du Fg-St-Denis)*
> *Phone: 01/47.70.13.59*
> *Fax: 01/42.47.00.80*
> *Open daily until 1:30 a.m.*
>
> Alsatian food and Parisian atmosphere at this 1886 *brasserie,* on a passageway in an area not frequented by tourists. Jam-packed with some of the strangest people you'll see in Paris, and getting there's half the fun. Moderate. ❖

⁖

11ᵗʰ Arrondissement

The 11ᵗʰ, centered on the Bastille, is primarily a residential area that has become increasingly hip lately, especially around rue de Charonne and rue de Lappe.

place de la Bastille/Opéra Bastille
11ᵗʰ/Métro Bastille
East end of rue St-Antoine

Let's go see the Bastille! Well, you won't find it here. The notorious Bastille prison was torn down over 200 years ago when mobs stormed the Bastille as part of the French Revolution. Today, it's a roundabout traffic circle where cars speed around the 170-foot **July Column**. You come here for the wonderful cafés. You'll also find the **Bastille Opera House (Opéra Bastille)** on the south side of the place. Opened in 1989, this modern glass building hosts opera and symphony performances. Phone: 01/04.01.17.89 for tickets.

TIP: Want to get tickets to events before you leave home? Globaltickets of New York, 800/223-6108, will mail tickets to you to the opera, symphony, special events and tourist attractions before you leave for Paris. There's about a 25% surcharge.

Art galleries exhibiting the work of contemporary artists are found along rue de Lappe, rue de Charonne and Rue Keller.

THE BEST CHOCOLATE
SHOP IN PARIS!
A la Petite Fabrique
11ᵗʰ/Métro Bastille or Bréguet Sabin
12 rue St-Sabin
Phone: 01/48.05.82.02
Closed Sun. and Mon.

This small and unpretentious chocolate shop near the place de la Bastille has excellent chocolates that make great gifts and are easy to pack to take home. ⁖

Edith Piaf Museum (Musée Edith Piaf)
11ᵗʰ/Métro Ménilmontant
5 rue Crespin-du-Gast
Phone: 01/43.55.52.72
by appointment only
Admission: Free

If you're a fan of "The Little Sparrow," the voice behind *La Vie en Rose* and countless other songs by the most famous Parisian *chanteuse*, you'll want to visit her apartment. Her sheet

RESTAURANTS TIP

The 11th is home to some of the most interesting and diverse dining experiences in Paris. Here are just a few that you could try:

Auberge Pyrénnées-Cévennes
11th/Métro République
106 rue de la Folie-Méricourt
Phone: 01/43.57.33.78
Closed Sat. (lunch) and Sun.

Small, charming restaurant serving the food of Southwest France. Hams hanging from the ceiling add to the charm. Try the *cassoulet*. Moderate.

Le Souk
11th/Métro Bastille
1 rue Keller
Phone: 01/49.29.05.08
Closed Mon.

This attractive, popular Moroccan restaurant is always busy and the interior is exotic. Good selection of vegetarian dishes. Moderate.

Pause Café
11th/Métro Ledru-Rollin
41 rue de Charonne
Phone: 01/48.06.80.33

Popular café specializing in *tourtes*. Inexpensive.

Bistro Paul-Bert
11th/Métro Faidherbe-Chaligny
18 rue Paul-Bert
Phone: 01/43.72.24.01
Closed Sun. and Mon.

A truly neighborhood bistro experience from its traditional décor to its menu written on a blackboard. Inexpensive.

Chardenoux
11th/Métro Charonne
1 rue Jules-Vallès and 23 rue Chanzy
Phone: 01/43.71.49.52
Fax: 01/45.62.04.07

Traditional Parisian cooking in the Bastille/République area. This small and friendly restaurant has been in business for almost 100 years. Moderate.

Chez Paul
11th/Métro Bastille
13 rue de Charonne
Phone: 01/47.00.34.57

My favorite bistro in Paris. Never a bad meal (try the rabbit), and ask to eat upstairs. The service can be very Parisian, if you know what I mean. Moderate.

music, clothes, fan letters and concert posters are all here. While you tour the small museum, you'll hear her recordings. The apartment is not too far from her grave at the Père-Lachaise cemetery.

The Smoking Museum
(Musée du Fumeur)
11th/Métro Voltaire
7 rue Pache

Phone: 01/46.59.05.51
Closed Sun. (morning) and Mon.
Admission: Free

Only in Paris would there be a museum dedicated to all things related to smoking, from 17th-century clay pipes to works of art revolving around smoking to a greenhouse for tobacco plants. There's a gift shop and a café (and yes, you can smoke there).

12th Arrondissement

The 12th is home to the Gare de Lyon train station. This primarily residential area is bordered on the east by the Bois de Vincennes, a beautiful park.

Aquarium Tropical de la Porte Dorée
12th/Métro Porte Dorée
293 avenue Daumesnil
Phone: 01/44.74.84.80
Closed Tues.
Admission: 4€, under 14 free

Enjoy eighty terrariums and aquariums filled with flora and fauna from lakes, rivers and oceans of the Pacific Islands and Africa.

RESTAURANT TIP
Le Train Bleu
12th/Métro Gare-de-Lyon
In the Gare de Lyon train station.
20 boulevard Diderot
Phone: 01/43.43.09.06
Fax: 01/43.43.97.96

Forget all the food you've eaten in train stations. It's delicious here. But you don't really come here for the food anyway because the setting, with its murals of the French-speaking world, is spectacular. A great place to have a drink. Expensive. ✳

Bois de Vincennes
12th/Métro Château de Vincennes (you can also take the métro to Porte Dorée and then transfer to bus 46)
Eastern edge of Paris

Past the medieval castle, **Château de Vincennes** (Phone: 01/48.08.31.20, open daily. Admission: 6€), is the **Bois de Vincennes** (woods) containing a beautiful floral park, the **Parc Floral** (Phone: 01/55.94.20.20, open daily. Admission: 3€). If you're interested in gardening, especially flowers, you'll enjoy viewing not only the seasonal flowers, but also the bamboo, bonsai, medicinal plants and ferns (all labeled with their latin names).

France's largest zoo, **Parc Zoologique** (Phone: 01/44.75.20.10, open daily, admission 8€), is also here.

~

13th Arrondissement

The 13th is a residential area, home to Chinatown and the grand National Library.

Bibliothèque Nationale de France
*13th/Métro Bibliothèque
quai François-Mauriac*
Phone: 01/53.79.59.59
Closed Mon.
Admission: Free

France's National Library, the pet project of former president François Mitterand, has four towers that were designed to represent open books (it's a library, after all). It has a wonderful bookstore, and there's a peaceful sunken courtyard.

Rue Louise-Weiss
13th/Métro Bibliothèque

This street can only be called "up and coming." There are now

RESTAURANT TIP
L'Avant Goût
13th/Métro place d'Italie
26 rue Bobillot
Phone: 01/53.80.24.00
Fax: 01/53.80.00.77
Closed Sun., Mon. and most of Aug. Reservations a must

Mix with the French in this small, crowded bistro near the place d'Italie. Consistently good cuisine and very French. Try the *pot-au-feu* (stew of meat and vegetables). Inexpensive-Moderate. ❖

at least 10 galleries here. After you've had enough gallery-hopping, visit the colossal, wedge-shaped **MK2 Bibliothèque** at 128/162 Ave. de France, in front of the Bibliothèque National de France. This modern complex has a cinema with 14 screens, a bar and three restaurants.

RESTAURANT TIP
Le Petit Marguery
13th/Métro Gobelins
9 boulevard de Port-Royal
Phone: 01/43.31.58.59
Closed Sun., Mon. and Aug.

Owned by brothers, this 1930s bistro features game dishes and is known for its good service. Moderate.

Manufacture des Gobelins
13th/Métro Gobelins
42 avenue des Gobelins
Phone: 01/44.08.52.00
Guided tours Tues. through Thurs.
at 2 p.m. (in French only)
Admission: 8€

Tours will guide you through how the famous Gobelin tapestries, dating back to the days of French royalty, were (and still are) made.

Chinatown
13th/Métro Tolbiac

The 13 square blocks around the Tolbiac métro stop is home to Paris's Chinatown. Chinatown doesn't look much like you would expect. It's a lot of tall, uninteresting buildings with Chinese shops (especially electronic and clothing) and restaurants. The area is densely populated. At the end of the Vietnam war, refugees moved here in droves. There are some good places to eat here if you have a hankering for authentic Chinese or Vietnamese food. One of the most interesting places is the Tang Supermarket at 48 avenue d'Ivry.

RESTAURANT TIP
Café Banal
13th/Métro Gobelins
30 boulevard de Port-Royal
Closed weekends

The owner has a mission: to serve good food at reasonable prices. Salads, omelets, ham and cheese sandwiches and chicken dishes all cost about 1.50€ per dish. Phillippe Leclerq, the owner, thinks that a full meal should cost less than minimum wage. Sort of like an American diner, but with a French twist. Yes, they do serve wine and alcohol. By the way, *banal* means *ordinary* in French.

~

14th and 15th Arrondissements

Known as Montparnasse and centered around the lively boulevard Montparnasse (once the center of Paris's avant-garde scene), these areas are primarily residential.

Cimetière du Montparnasse
14th/Métro Edgar Quinet
Enter on either rue Froidevaux or boulevard Edgar Quinet off of boulevard Raspail.
Admission: Free

This quiet but somewhat messy cemetery is the "permanent home" of Samuel Beckett, Jean-Paul Sartre, Simone de Beauvoir and other celebrities of the past. Located near the Tour Montparnasse.

Les Catacombes
14th/Métro Denfert-Rochereau
1 place Denfert-Rochereau
Phone: 01/43.22.47.63
Closed Mon.
Admission: 5€, under 7 free

Grim, strange and claustrophobic. Beginning in the late 1700s, six million people were deposited in what used to be stone quarries. It gets even creepier. The bones are arranged in patterns. Not for everyone.

Musée Lenine
14th/Métro Alésia
4 rue Marie-Rose
Phone: 01/42.79.99.58
Open by appointment only
Admission: Free (of course)

A sort of mecca for world communists, this museum is where Lenin resided in Paris from 1909 to 1912.

> ### RESTAURANT TIP
> ### La Closerie des Lilas
> *14th/Métro Vavin*
> *171 boulevard du Montparnasse*
> *Phone: 01/40.51.34.50*
>
> And if you didn't get enough of Lenin at his museum, drop by the historic café where he and Trotsky and many other famous people hung out. There's a terrace, piano bar, *brasserie* (moderate) and restaurant (expensive). Moderate-Expensive. ❊

Fondation Cartier
14th/Métro Raspail
261 boulevard Raspail
Phone: 01/42.18.56.51

5th, 6th, 13th, 14th and 15th Arrondissements

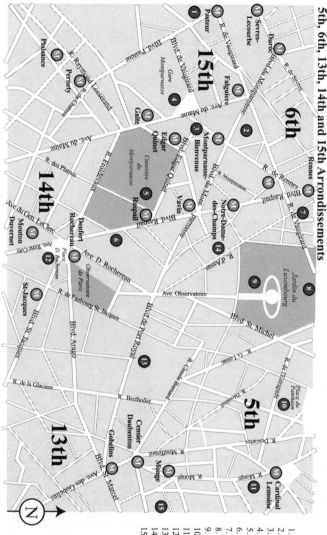

1. Musée Pasteur
2. Musée Bourdelle
3. Tour Montparnasse
4. Gare Montparnasse
5. Cimetière du Montparnasse
6. Fondation Cartier
7. St-Joseph-des-Carmes
8. Palais du Luxembourg
9. Jardins du Luxembourg
10. Panthéon
11. Arènes de Lutèce
12. Les Catacombs
13. Val-de-Grâce
14. Musée Zadkine
15. Mosquée de Paris

Ⓜ Métro Stop

Closed Mon.
Admission: 7€

This contemporary art and photography museum is housed in an incredible glass building.

Musée Adzak
14ᵗʰ/Métro Plaisance
3 rue Jonquoy
Phone: 01/45.43.06.98
By appointment only
Admission: Free

This museum is devoted to the works of British pop artist Roy Adzak who was known for his photography and molds of the human body.

Montparnasse Tower
(Tour Montparnasse)
15ᵗʰ/Métro Montparnasse-Bienvenüe
Closed weekends in the winter
Admission: 7€

This unfortunate 1970s black glass tower that dominates its Left Bank neighbors has an observation deck. Take the elevator to the 56ᵗʰ floor and then steps to the roof. There was such outrage after this tower was built that an ordinance was passed prohibiting further towers in the city center.

Musée Pasteur
15ᵗʰ/Métro Pasteur
25 rue du Docteur Roux
Phone: 01/45.68.82.83

Closed Sat., Sun. and Aug.
Admission: 3€

The apartment of Louis Pasteur has been converted into a museum dedicated to preserving the memory of his work. His discovery that most infectious diseases are caused by germs is one of the most important in medical history. The Pasteur Institute headquartered here continues its research into infectious diseases. Did you know that Wallace Simpson gave the institute her famous jewelry collection when she died in 1993?

Postal Museum
(Musée de la Poste)
15ᵗʰ/Métro Pasteur or Montparnasse-Bienvenüe
34 boulevard de Vaugirard
Phone: 01/42.79.24.24
Closed Sun.
Admission: 5€, under 12 free

This museum is devoted to French and international philately (stamp collections).

Musée Bourdelle
15ᵗʰ/Métro Montparnasse-Bienvenüe or Falguière
16-18 rue Antoine Bourdelle
Phone: 01/49.54.73.73
Closed Mon.
Admission: Permanent collection is free. 5€ for exhibits

Bourdelle was a student of Rodin and if you're a fan of sculpture,

RESTAURANTS TIP

La Coupole
14th/Métro Vavin
102 boulevard Montparnasse
Phone: 01/43.20.14.20
Fax: 01/43.35.46.14

Hang out where Picasso hung out! A Montparnasse institution since the days of Picasso, this noisy *brasserie* is a favorite among tourists. It's known for its oysters. The atmosphere is "belle époque." Moderate.

Le Flamboyant
14th/Métro Pernety
11 rue Boyer-Barret
Phone: 01/45.41.00.22
Closed Sun. and Mon.

If you're a fan of Caribbean food, this is a great French West Indian restaurant, though it's a bit of a trip. There are so few tourists who come here that the owner is not quite sure what to do with you, but the food is great, especially considering the price. Inexpensive.

Je Thé...Me
15th/Métro Vaugirard
4 rue d'Alleray
Phone: 01/48.42.48.30
Closed Sun., Mon. and Aug.

This attractive bistro is in a century-old grocery store and serves classic French fare. Moderate.

Le Dix Vin
15th/Métro Pasteur
57 rue Falguière
Phone: 01/43.20.91.77
Closed Sun. and Mon.
No credit cards

Neighborhood wine bar with solid, reasonably priced food and wine. You'll find traditional Parisian bistro fare served by attentive waiters in an area not frequented by most tourists. Moderate.

Bistro 121
15th/Métro Boucicaut
121 rue de la Convention
Phone: 01/45.57.52.90
Fax: 01/45.57.14.69
Occasionally closed on Mon.

A favorite of many seeking a romantic, elegant evening in a classic French bistro. Try the *poulet fermier* (free-range chicken). Moderate.

Le Tire-Bouchon
15th/Métro Charles-Michels
62 rue des Entrepreneurs
Phone: 01/40.59.09.27
Closed Sun., Mon. (lunch) and Sat. (lunch)

Named after the corkscrew, this small restaurant serves good food at reasonable prices. Moderate. ❖

you won't want to miss this museum in a residential area of Montparnasse. Bourdelle's famous 21 studies of Beethoven are housed here.

Maison de la Culture du Japon
15th/Métro Bir-Hakeim
101 bis Quai Branly
Phone: 01/44.37.95.00
Closed Sun. and Mon.
Admission: 5€

Celebrates Japanese culture with changing exhibits.

Aquaboulevard
15th/Métro Porte de Versailles or Balard
4 rue Louis-Armand
Phone: 01/40.60.10.00
Open daily
Admission: 20€ (family passes at reduced price)

Kids will love this huge water park and sports center. Wave pools, water slides, tennis courts, golf range and a food court. No matter what your age or size, all men are required to wear speedo-type swimsuits. What's that all about?

17th Arrondissement

CHEESE SHOPS
Cheese is like gold to the French. Charles de Gaulle is reported to have said "How can anyone govern a nation that has 246 different kinds of cheese?" Two wonderful cheese shops (*fromageries*) in the 17th are:

Alléosse
17th/Métro Ternes
13 rue Poncelet
Phone: 01/42.96.08.66
Closed Mon.

Alléosse serves rare cheeses from throughout France.

Androuët sur le Pouce
17th/Métro Villiers
23 rue du Villiers
Phone: 01/47.64.39.20

Large cheese shop. This organization also operates a *bar à fromage* (cheese bar) at 49 rue St-Roch (1st/ Métro Pyramides).

The Arc de Triomphe and beautiful Parc Monceau border the residential 17th.

Musée Henner
17th/Métro Malesherbes
43 avenue de Villiers
Phone: 01/47.63.42.73
Closed Mon.
Admission: 5€, under 18 free

This national museum is devoted to the works of Jean-Jacques Henner. Who? Henner was an Alsatian painter of note in the 19th century. Come here if you're interested in paintings of the Romantic era (you know, paintings with lots of nymphs).

∽

18th Arrondissement

Once a small village of vineyards and windmills, Montmartre is dominated by the massive Sacred Heart Basilica. It's also home to the sleazy place Pigalle and the largest flea market in Paris.

The **place des Abbesses** is a picturesque triangular "square" and features one of the few remaining curvy Art Nouveau entrances to the Abbesses métro stop. This métro stop is the deepest in Paris and stands on the site of a medieval abbey.

Sacred Heart Basilica
(Basilique du Sacré-Coeur)
18th/Métro Anvers or Abbesses
place Parvis-du-Sacré-Coeur
Open daily

Admission: Free. To the observation deck in the dome (and to the crypt) is 5€

To avoid climbing the hundreds of steps to the Basilica, you can take the métro to Abbesses, then take the elevator and follow the signs to the funicular (cable car), which will take you up to the Basilica for the price of a métro ticket. For directions, see the Montmartre walk in this book.

At the top of the hill (*butte*) in Montmartre is the Basilica of the Sacred Heart which wasn't completed until 1919. The Basilica is named for Christ's sacred heart which some believe is in the crypt. You can't miss the Basilica with its white onion

18th Arrondissement (Montmartre)

1. place des Abbesses
2. Basilique du Sacré Coeur
3. Eglise St-Pierre
4. place du Terre
5. Espace Salvador-Dali
6. Musée du Vieux Montmartre
7. Montmartre Vineyard
8. Au Lapin Agile
9. Musée d'Art Juif
10. Square Suzanne Buisson
11. Moulin de la Galette
12. Windmill
13. Bateau-Lavoir/
    Four Graces Fountain
14. Bar-tabac des Deux Moulins
15. Moulin Rouge
16. Cimetière de Montmartre
17. Musée d'Art Max Fourny/
    Halle St-Pierre

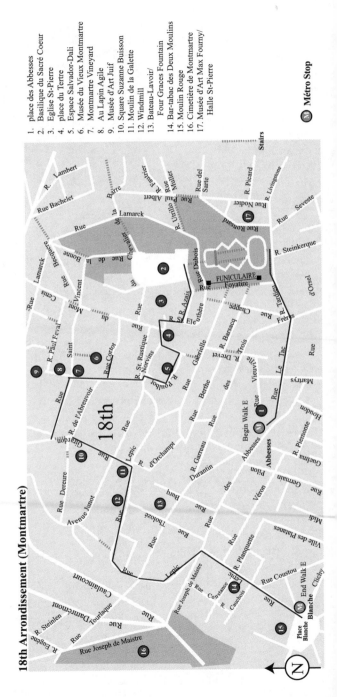

domes and Byzantine and Romanesque architecture. Inside you'll find gold mosaics, but the real treat is the view of Paris from the dome.

Musée d'Art Max Fourny
18th/Métro Anvers
2 rue Ronsard
Phone: 01/42.58.72.89
Open daily
Admission: 6€

This museum is located at the foot of Sacré-Coeur and displays temporary exhibitions of folk/naive art from around the world. A must for folk-art aficionados.

Halle St-Pierre
18th/Métro Anvers
2 rue Ronsard (at the bottom of the hill on the right as you face the Sacred Heart Basilica)

This former 19th-century market hall is now home to the Max Fourny museum (above), exhibit space, a café and shopss.

Rue Foyatier
18th/Métro Anvers or Abbesses

With over 200 steps, this "street" is west (left) of the hill leading up to Sacré-Coeur. It is one of the most photographed streets in Paris.

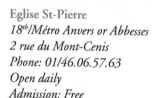

RESTAURANT TIP
Café L'Été en Pente Douce
18th/Métro Château-Rouge
23 rue Muller
Phone: 01/42.64.02.67

Interesting and picturesque café near Sacré-Coeur. Inexpensive. ❊

Eglise St-Pierre
18th/Métro Anvers or Abbesses
2 rue du Mont-Cenis
Phone: 01/46.06.57.63
Open daily
Admission: Free

One of the oldest churches in Paris in the shadows of Sacré-Coeur. The Roman marble columns date back to the 1100s.

The **place du Tertre** is east of Sacré-Coeur. It's filled with tourists and artists trying to paint your portrait.

Espace Salvador-Dali
18th/Métro Abbesses
11 rue Poulbot
Phone: 01.42.64.40.10
Open daily
Admission: 7€

Black walls, weird music with Dali's voice and dim lighting all make this museum of the works of Salvador Dali an interesting experience. Come here if you're a fan of his work to see 300 lithographs and etchings and 25 sculptures.

Four Graces Fountain
18th/Métro Abbesses
place Emile-Goudeau

Halfway up the Montmartre hill is a green-painted fountain. At the end of the 19th century, English art collector Richard Wallace donated hundreds of these fountains to the city. He thought it was unfair that there was nowhere in Paris that you could get a free drink of water (you had to pay for it in a café).

Bateau-Lavoir
18th/Métro Abbesses
13 place Emile-Goudeau

A replica of the house that was once home to some of the world's greatest artists, including Picasso and Modigliani, is here.

Musée du Vieux Montmartre
18th/Métro Anvers
12 rue Cortot
Phone: 01/46.06.61.11
Closed Mon.
Admission: 4€

Renoir and van Gogh are just a few of the artists who have occupied this 17th-century house. It's now a museum with a collection of mementos of this neighborhood, including paintings, posters and photographs.

> **ENTERTAINMENT TIP**
> **Au Lapin Agile/Cabaret des Assassins**
> *18th/Métro Lamarck-Caulaincourt*
> *Intersection of rue des Saules and rue St-Vincent*
> *Phone: 01/46.06.85.87*
> *Closed Mon.*
> *Admission: 25€ (includes a drink)*
>
> You'll likely hear French folk tunes coming out of this shuttered cottage at the picturesque intersection of rue des Saules and rue St-Vincent. It was once frequented by Picasso. Today, you'll sit at small wooden tables and listen to *chansonniers* (singers). Truly a Parisian experience. ❋

The last remaining **vineyard** in Paris is at the corner of rue St-Vincent and rue des Saules near the place Jules Joffrin (18th/Métro Lamarck-Caulaincourt). They still sell wine here. The labels are designed by local artists. The harvesting of the grapes in October gives the residents of Montmartre one more excuse to have a festival.

Musée d'Art Juif
18th/Métro Lamarck-Caulaincourt
42 rue des Saules
Phone: 01/42.57.84.15

Closed. Fri., Sat. and Aug.
Admission: 5€

A museum of ancient and modern Jewish art.

In the 19th century, Montmartre had many vineyards and over 40 windmills. One surviving windmill is the **Moulin de la Galette** on the corner of rue Girardon and rue Lepic. If it looks familiar, it's the windmill portrayed by Renoir in his painting of the same name. There is another windmill down the street at the corner of rue Lepic and rue Tholozé.

BISTRO AND MOVIE SITE
The movie "Amélie" won not only many film awards, but also a cult following. The lead character is a waitress. You can visit Amélie's 1950s bistro **Bar-tabac des Deux Moulins** at 15 rue Lepic, 18th/Métro Blanche, where you'll find mostly locals enjoying good homemade desserts and standard bistro fare. ❀

Cimetière de Montmartre
18th/Métro place de Clichy or Blanche
20 avenue Rachel (north of boulevard de Clichy)
Open daily
Admission: Free

Painter Degas, composer Berlioz and others are buried here on the Montmartre slope. Not as impressive as the huge Père-Lachaise cemetery in the 20th.

ENTERTAINMENT TIP
Moulin Rouge
18th/Métro Blanche
82 boulevard de Clichy
Phone: 01/53.09.82.82
Open nightly
Admission: begins at 85€

You've seen the movie, now see the cancan. Originally a red windmill, this dance hall has been around since 1889. It's without a doubt the most famous cabaret in the world. Toulouse-Lautrec memorialized the Moulin Rouge in his paintings. Looking for a little bit of Vegas? You'll find it here.

A fun curiosity just behind the Moulin Rouge is the "Love Wall" where "I love you" is written in a zillion languages. ❀

---

place Pigalle
18th/Métro Pigalle
Eastern end of boulevard de Clichy

You come here for only one thing: sex. Littered with sex shops, this area was known as "Pig Alley" during World War

II. During the day, neighborhood residents walking with their children and eating ice cream, seem oblivious to all the sex shops, reminding us that this is, after all, just another Paris neighborhood.

Montmartretrain
18th/Métro Pigalle
Admission: 4€

This tourist train departs from the place Pigalle up the hill to the Sacred Heart Basilica (with stops at many attractions). The tour takes about 40 minutes.

L'Étoile d'Or
9th/Métro Pigalle
30 rue Fontaine
Phone: 01/48.74.59.55
Closed Mon. morning and Sun.

Amid the sex shops of Pigalle, you'll find an incredible candy shop. The tiny shop's windows are plastered with praise from food writers from around the world. The interior dates back to the early 1900s. Among the wooden drawers and antique mirrors are some of the best candy concoctions you could ever imagine. The gift boxes are great to take home.

Museum of Erotic Art
(Musée de l'Erotisme)
18th/Métro Blanche
72 blvd. de Clichy
Phone: 01.42.58.28.73
Open daily
Admission: 7€

This museum is devoted to erotic art. 2,000 paintings, photos, carvings (can you say "dildo"?), implements ... Well, you get the picture. Not surprisingly, the museum remains open until the wee hours of the morning. There's also a "gift" shop, of course.

Clignancourt Flea Market
18th/Métro Porte de Clignancourt
(turn left, then cross the boulevard Nay)
Open Sat-Mon. 9 a.m.-7 p.m.

This is the **Marché aux Puces** ("flea market"), the most famous flea market in Paris. When you get off at the métro stop, just follow the crowds. Work your way through the junk on the outskirts of the market (watch your wallet) until you find the interesting antique dealers around rue des Rosiers and avenue Michelet. You can find all sorts of small souvenirs to take home. If you get hungry, there are cheap snack stands and a few good restaurants. Some think the **Marché aux Puces de la Porte de Vanves** in the 14th/Métro Porte de Vanves is better for purchases, but definitely has less atmosphere (open Sat. and Sun.).

~

19th Arrondissement

This diverse residential area is home to the futuristic Parc de la Vilette.

Musée de la Musique
19th/Métro Porte de Pantin
221 avenue Jean-Jaurès
Phone: 01/44.84.44.84
Closed Mon.
Admission: 10€, under 18 free

Located in the **Cité de la Musique** (the $120 million stone-and-glass part of the Parc de la Villette), this museum features over 4,000 musical instruments from Baroque Italy to present-day France. You'll be given a headset (available in English). As you stroll through the museum, every time you approach an exhibit, the headset begins to play the music of that instrument. Very entertaining for kids and adults.

Parc des Buttes Chaumont
19th/Métro Botzaris
rue Manin

Created in 1867 (from a former garbage dump), this peaceful park has artificial cliffs, streams, waterfalls and jogging paths.

RESTAURANT TIP
La Cave Gourmande
19th/Métro Danube or Botzaris
10 rue du Général-Brunet
Phone: 01/40.40.03.30 (also fax)
Closed Sun., Mon. and Aug.

Raves for the cuisine, but not for the trip out to this "remote" part of Paris. "Foodies" love this place and I had one of the best meals of my life here. Moderate-Expensive. ❀

City of Science and Industry
(Cité des Sciences et de l'Industrie)
19th/Métro Porte de La Villette
At the northern edge of the city in the Parc de La Villette
30 avenue Corentine-Cariou
Phone: 01/40.05.80.00
Closed Mon.
Admission: 8€, under 7 free (separate 9€ admission for La Géode)

Huge and spectacular museum dedicated to science and industry, including a geodesic dome (**La Géode**), a planetarium, aquarium, a submarine and much more. The futuristic **Parc de La Villette** is more than just a park. It features gardens and paths, but also has modern sculptures and bizarre park benches. A great place for kids. On certain summer evenings, films are shown for free on huge outdoor screens. For years, this was the site of the city's slaughterhouses.

20th Arrondissement

The 20th is dominated by the Cimetière du Père-Lachaise. Another diverse neighborhood.

Cimetière du Père-Lachaise
20th/Métro Père-Lachaise
Enter off the boulevard de Menilmontant.
Free maps available at the main entrance when a guard is on duty.

In 1626, the Jesuits opened a retreat for retired priests on this site. Father (Père) Lachaise, Louis XIV's confessor, visited here often. The Jesuits were expelled in 1763 and the city bought the property (all 110 acres) and converted it into a cemetery. It's the largest cemetery in Paris and is the eternal home to an incredible list of people, including Maria Callas, Chopin, Oscar Wilde, Balzac, Bellini, Proust, Modigliani, Gertrude Stein and Edith Piaf. Oh yeah, Jim Morrison of the Doors is buried here, too (as you can tell by the hoards of fans and graffiti near his grave, which has become a pilgrimage for his admirers. The graves range from simple, unadorned headstones to elaborate monuments and chapels.

Despite the fact that you're wandering in a cemetery, the grounds are quite beautiful and there are over 3,000 trees here. Each family is responsible for the upkeep of the family plot, and some are in extreme states of disrepair. There's a new 30-year-lease policy in place, so if the family doesn't renew the lease, the remains can be removed. It's believed that Jim Morrison's lease will never expire, much to the dismay of families who have their plots nearby.

If you enter the cemetery from the back off of rue des Rondeaux, you'll find the **Jardin du Souvenir**, with a series of stark, heart-wrenching memorials and tombstones dedicated to those who died in military combat or concentration camps during World War II.

RESTAURANT TIP
La Boulangerie
20ʰ/Métro Ménilmontant
15 rue des Panoyaux
Phone: 01/43.58.45.45
Closed Sat. (lunch) and Sun.

A classic French bistro located in a former bakery in the increasingly trendy Ménilmontant area near Père-Lachaise cemetery. Moderate. ❋

Off the Beaten Path

Veterinary Museum
(Musée Fragonard d'Alfort)
In the suburb of Maisons-Alfort/
Métro Alfort-Ecole Vétérinaire
Located in the National Veteri-
nary School
Phone: 01/43.96.71.72
Open Tues. and Wed. afternoons
and weekends. Closed Aug.
Admission: 3.50€

Ugh! Animal skeletons, skinned cats, a camel's stomach and a partially flayed 200-year-old horse and its rider are just some of the rather grim exhibits at this veterinary school.

Basilique de St-Denis
Métro Basilique St-Denis (near
the end of line 13)
1 rue de la Légion d'Honneur
Phone: 01/48.09.83.54

Open daily
Admission: 5€ (to the tombs and choir)

Saint Denis, the first bishop of Paris, was the patron saint of the monarchs. Decapitated by a king who thought he had too much influence, he's depicted on the front of Notre-Dame (holding his head in his hands). This is France's first Gothic building. You come here to see the royal tombs. Henri II and Catherine de Médicis, Louis XII and Anne de Bretagne, and Louis XVI and Marie Antoinette are all buried here along with other royals. The heart of Louis XVII, the son of Louis XVI and Marie Antoinette, was recently placed in the royal crypt. Who keeps these things? If you like history, especially history of the royals, this is a must.

La Défense
Métro Grande Arche de La Défense
Parvis de La Défense
Phone: 01/49.07.27.57
Open daily

The future is here. While most of Paris is void of tall, modern skyscrapers, La Défense is the home to many modern, interesting office buildings. The crown jewel is the huge **Grande Arche de La Défense**, a modern arch aligned with the (tiny, by comparison) Arc de Triomphe. You could fit Notre-Dame under it. Glass tube elevators can take you to the top for 7€.

Dog Cemetery
(Cimetière des Chiens)
In the Asnières-sur-Siene suburb/
Métro Pont de Clichy
4 Pont de Clichy (on the river)
Phone: 01/40.86.24.11
Open mid-March to mid-October. Closed Tues.

The French love their dogs (and cats) so much that they have an entire cemetery with some elaborate memorials to countless poodles and even Rin Tin Tin. Lots of stray cats make this run-down cemetery their home. How totally French!

Excursions

Versailles
Take the RER train line C (from métro stops St-Michel, Gare d'Austerlitz, Invalides, Musée d'Orsay, Pont de l'Alma, Javel or Champ de Mars) to Versailles-Rive Gauche. 40-minute trip. 5€ round-trip. There's a shuttle bus (2€), but the château is a short walk.
You can also reach Versailles by SNCF trains from Gare St-Lazare and Gare-Montparnasse (10-minute walk to the château).
Phone: 01/30.83.78.00
The château is closed Mon.

Admission: 7.50€ (plus 4.50€ if you take a guided tour)

The "Sun King" Louis XIV began construction of his opulent château in 1664. The highlights of your trip include the opulent Hall of Mirrors, the baroque Royal Chapel (Chapelle Royale), the ornate queen's bedroom, the marble courtyard, the royal apartments, an opera house, and the Throne Room (Salon d'Apollon). The famous gardens are especially beautiful in summer (especially weekends at around 3:30 p.m.) when the Dragon Fountain and Fountain of Neptune (along with many other fountains) gush water. (Admission: 3€. Gardens open daily). The gardens also contain the miniature palace, the Grand Trianon and the beautiful mansion, the Petit Trianon. There is also the picturesque and charming **Hamlet** where Marie Antoinette used to pretend that she was a peasant. Royalty!

Disneyland Paris

Take the RER line A (from many métro stops such as Nation, Châtelet-Les Halles or Charles-de-Gaulle-Étoile) to Marne-la Vallée/ Chessy. 45-minute trip. Fare is 13€ round-trip. Phone: 01/ 60.30.60.30
One-day admission to Disneyland is 30-40€ for adults, 25-30€ under age 13 and free under 4. Package deals available.
www.disneylandparis.com

The biggest tourist attraction in France (even greater than the Eiffel Tower), Disneyland Paris isn't much different than the Disney parks in the U.S. Main Street USA, Adventureland, Frontierland, Fantasyland and Discoveryland are all here. **Village Disney** is a free entertainment area with restaurants, bars and clubs. **Walt Disney Studios** (an interactive film studio) is next to Disneyland (separate admission charge).

Giverny: Claude Monet House and Garden

(Maison et Jardin de Claude Monet)
Trains depart Gare-St-Lazare to Vernon (the Paris-Rouen train). 50-minute trip. About 15€ round-trip. 3 miles from the train station by taxi or bus.
Phone: 02/32.51.28.21
Open Apr.-Oct. Closed Mon.
Admission: 6€, under 7 free

French Impressionist painter Claude Monet lived here for 43 years and painted, among other things, the water lilies and Japanese bridges found in the beautiful gardens. Monet's green-shuttered house is now a museum. Nearby is the **American Art Museum (Musée d'Art Americain)** dedicated to U.S.-born Impressionist artists:
Admission: 5€, under 11 free
Open Apr.-Oct. Closed Mon.
Phone: 02/32.51.94.65

Chartres

Trains from Gare Montparnasse to Chartres. About an hour trip. About 15€ round-trip.
Phone: 02/37.28.15.58
Admission: Free
Malcolm Miller conducts excellent tours in English for 7€.

The gothic **Cathédrale Notre-Dame de Chartres** with its two tall spires, world-famous stained glass windows and its three sculpted doorways (Royal Portal) is a popular day trip from Paris. The picturesque old town (**Vieux Quartier**) is quite different from bustling Paris.

Rambouillet

Trains depart Gare Montparnasse every 30 minutes. 35-minute trip. Round-trip fare is 15€. Phone: 01/34.83.21.21 (tourist office) Closed Tues.
Admission: 6€, under 11 free

The **Forest of Rambouillet** is 47,000 acres and is home to the **Château de Rambouillet**. The castle, which dates back to the 1300s, is known for its elaborate woodwork and huge tapestries. Before his exile, Napoleon spent his last night here.

Fontainebleau

Trains depart Gare de Lyon. A 50-60 minute trip. 15€ round-trip. The palace is 1-1/2 miles from the train station. A bus runs every 15-30 minutes from the station (2€). Tickets including train, bus fare and admission cost 20€ and are available at Gare de Lyon. Phone: 01/60.74.99.99 (tourist office)
Closed on Tues.
Admission: 6€, under 18 free

The French monarchy used this as a resort and for hunting in its forest. Like Versailles, it's a study in excess, but it's not as grand as Versailles. Highlights include the elegant ballroom, the golden Throne Room, the elaborate Louis XV staircase and the Gallery of François I. The gardens are also not as grand as Versailles, but certainly beautiful to stroll in.

Chantilly

Trains from Gare du Nord daily. 30-minute trip. You can walk to the château or take a cab or bus, which is one mile away. Phone: 03/44.62.62.62 The château is closed on Tues. during Nov.- Feb. Admission: 7€, under 18 free www.chateaudechantilly.com

Chantilly makes for a relaxing day trip from Paris. The picturesque village of Chantilly is the site of the magnificent **Château de Chantilly**, which dates back to the 1600s and was restored in the 19th century. It's the home of the **Condé Museum (Musée Condé)**, known for its tapestries. Horse lovers will want to visit the **Great Stables (Grand Écuries)** and its **Horse Museum (Musée Vivant du Cheval:** *Phone: 03/44.57.40.40 Closed Tues. Admission: 8€.*

Vaux-le-Vicomte

Trains depart from Gare de Lyon to Melun (the same trains that run to Fontainebleau). Vaux-le-

Vicomte is 13 miles north of Fontainebleau. It's a 4-mile taxi ride from the train station at Melun.
Phone: 01/64.14.41.90
Open daily Easter to Nov.
Admission: 10€

Nicolas Fouquet, the finance minister to France in the mid 1600s, built this beautiful *château*. It's said that when Louis XIV visited, he soon had the finance minister arrested and then stole his art treasures. Louis XIV then used the planners of this *château* to build Versailles (on a larger scale). The garden is filled with statues, fountains and waterfalls, and is the site of special events such as impressive candlelight tours. A calendar of these special events is found at www.vaux-le-vicomte.com.

2. WALKS

ISLANDS WALK

Walk A. See map on page 11. (Highlights: Notre-Dame, Ste-Chapelle, Deportation Memorial and Ile St-Louis).

Your walk begins by taking the métro to the Pont Neuf stop.

Start your day with a beautiful view of all of Paris by heading over to **La Samaritaine** department store at 19 rue de la Monnaie. You'll be in front of the store when you get out of the métro. Have coffee and a chocolate croissant at the café. Even if you don't eat there, you can still take the elevator to the 9th floor and the steps to the 10th, and treat yourself to a great free view of the Paris skyline. I prefer to take the escalators up. That way you can see the incredible interior of this historic department store. Note that during certain times of the year, especially during winter, the outdoor café is closed. Other cafés on the upper floors also provide great views.

Now, head back down to the street level.

Along the Seine River on quai de la Mégisserie (between rue des Bourdonnais and place du Châtelet) you can wander through beautiful **plant stores** and **pet shops** (birds, puppies, fish, roosters, you name it) that spill out onto the sidewalks. You'll love this little strip of Paris.

When you reach **place du Châtelet**, take in the **Fountain of the Palms**. It was ordered by Napoleon to commemorate his victories in Egypt.

Turn to your right and cross the bridge.

The **Pont-au-Change** got its name because moneychangers used to have their booths on this bridge crossing the Seine River.

On the other side of the Pont-au-Change is the boulevard du Palais.

On the corner, look up and you'll see a fabulous 1334 Baroque **clock tower** (it still works), the first public clock in Paris. You're now on the **Ile de la Cité**, an island in the Seine River.

Continue down the boulevard du Palais.

On your right is the entrance to the **Musée de la Conciergerie**, a 14th-century prison where over 2,600 people waited to have their heads chopped off, including Marie Antoinette, during the French revolution's "Reign of Terror." If you have limited time, skip this museum and head down the street.

The Gothic palace that houses this museum along with the massive **Palais de Justice** were once part of the Palais de la Cité, the home of French kings. Today, it's home to the city's courts of law. You can watch the courts in session and view its beautiful interior for free. Closed Sun.

As you pass the gates to the palace, on your right, you'll see the entrance to our next stop.

If it's a sunny day, you cannot miss **la Ste-Chapelle**. You'll be dazzled by nearly 6,600 square feet of stained glass at this Gothic masterpiece. The walls are almost entirely stained glass. Fifteen windows depict biblical scenes from the Garden of Eden to the Apocalypse (the large rose window). The chapel was built in 1246 to house what some believe to be the Crown of Thorns, a nail from the crucifixion and other relics.

Cross the boulevard du Palais to rue de Lutèce.

Soon you'll see, to your left, the curvy, Art Nouveau Cité métro stop. You're now in the **place Louis-Lépine**. To your left is a lovely flower market (**Marché aux Fleurs**). On Sundays, the market becomes a bird market (**Marché aux Oiseaux**) where all types of birds, supplies and cages are sold.

Continue on and turn right at rue de la Cité.

Head down rue de la Cité to the square in front of Notre-Dame (**place du Parvis Notre-Dame**). It's the center of all of France. The bronze plaque on the ground outside the cathedral is "Point Zéro" from which all distances in France are measured. You'll also find the entry to the **Crypte Archéologique** here with ruins of Roman Paris. Head into **Notre-Dame** and admire this incredible structure.

As you exit the cathedral (with the cathedral to your back) head left and then make a left turn before the bridge.

Stroll through **Square Jean XXIII** along the river. Behind the cathedral is the lovely **Square de l'Ile de France**. Here you'll notice the "flying buttresses" that support Notre-Dame. From these squares, take in the beauty of Paris along the Seine River.

Directly behind the cathedral, cross the street (quai Archevêché) and head through the gate.

You'll now enter the **Deportation Memorial (Mémorial des Martyrs Français de la Déportation de 1945)**. It will take you only a short time to walk through this free memorial built in honor of the more than 30,000 citizens who were placed on boats at this spot for deportation to concentration camps. You descend steps and become surrounded by walls. Single-file, you enter a chamber. A hallway is covered with 200,000 crystals (one for each French citizen who died). At the far end of the hall is the eternal flame of hope. Don't miss this memorial. It's both moving and disturbing.

As you leave the memorial, exit out the gate, turn right on quai Archevêché. Head to the pedestrian bridge. Take a right onto the bridge.

You are now on the **Pont St-Louis**. There almost always are street musicians playing jazz to a crowd of onlookers.

Continue across this bridge to the Ile St-Louis.

The **Ile St-Louis** is a residential island within the city, often swamped with tourists during high season. The vast majority of the buildings on this island date back to the 1600s, making for a beautiful place to stroll, especially the small side streets. There are interesting shops and several good restaurants.

After you cross the bridge you'll be on the narrow **rue St-Louis-en-l'Ile**, one of the most beautiful streets in all of Paris. A few highlights on this street are:

• No. 81: **Oliviers and Co**. Stop at this lovely shop to buy olive oils and other products from around the Mediterranean.

• No. 78: **Boulangerie St-Louis**. A great bakery.

• No. 76: **La Ferme St-Aubin**. Stinky cheese from all over France.

• No. 69: **Mon Vieil Ami**. Popular and trendy bistro.

• No. 55: **L'Occitane**. All types of soaps from Provence.

• No. 51: **Kabrousse**. A great photo op as the flowers spill out onto the sidewalk at this florist.

> ## WHY ARE THESE AD-DRESSES NOT IN ORDER?
> Addresses in Paris are odd on one side of the street and even on the other, but they don't go in sequence. ❧

• No. 64: **Calixte**. Delicious *croissants* and other snacks. A great place to grab some stuff to eat in your hotel room or along the Seine.

• No. 51: **Hôtel de Chenizot**. Formerly the home of the archbishop, take a look at the beautiful and interesting balcony and doorway.

• No. 51: **L'Épicerie**. Gourmet food shop. Check out the chocolate snails.

• No. 54: **Hôtel du Jeu de Paume**. Antiques for sale next door to this historic hotel.

• No. 39: **Nos Ancêtres les Gaulois**. Interested in dining with other tourists? The waiters are humorously rude. Loads of fun. The food is not great, the menu is very limited, but you can have a fabulous time ... though it's definitely not for everyone. It's more of an experience than a dining experience. Get reservations; it's always crowded. Phone: 01/46.33.66.07.

• No. 31: **Berthillon**. Indulge at the best-known ice cream shop in Paris.

• No. 42: **Au Gourmet de l'Ile**. Busy bisto serving classic, moderately priced French bistro fare.

• No. 19: **Eglise St-Louis-en-l'Ile**. Construction of this church began in 1664 but wasn't completed until 1726. It has a beautiful ornate interior and an unusual iron clock on the outside.

• No. 26: **Librairie Ulysse**. Interesting travel bookstore. A good selection of Paris travel guides (in English), but the one you're reading now is really the only one you'll need.

• No. 24: **Galerie Bamyan**. Crafts from all over the world at this small shop.

• No. 24: **La Charlotte de l'Isle**. Another fantastic chocolate shop.

• No. 2: **Hotel Lambert**. Not much to look at anymore, this mansion was built in 1640 for President Lambert (known as Lambert the Rich).

At the end of the street, turn right and cross the bridge.

This bridge (**Pont Sully**) dates back to 1874 and is actually two independent steel bridges that extend from the Ile St-Louis to either side of the river. You're now on the Left Bank and can continue down the famous boulevard St-Germain-des-Prés.

You can head back to your hotel from any number of métro stops along the boulevard St-Germain-des-Prés.

LEFT BANK WALK

Walk B. See map on page 33. (Highlights: Musée Maillol, St-Germain-des-Prés, and the Luxembourg Gardens. Musée Maillol is closed on Tues.).

Take the métro to the rue du Bac stop.

When you get out of the métro, you'll be at the crossroads of rue du Bac, boulevard Raspail and boulevard St-Germain-des-Prés. On the corner is a typical Parisian café, the **Café St-Germain**. Why don't you start by having coffee and a croissant here? If you order *un café*, you'll get a small cup of very strong black coffee. If you'd like a larger cup of coffee with steamed milk, ask for *un crème*.

After you've had your wonderful Parisian coffee, you're going to visit one of the most interesting, if not the most bizarre, shops in Paris.

Cross rue Raspail and boulevard St-Germain-des-Prés to rue du Bac.

At 46 rue du Bac you'll find **Deyrolle**, a taxidermy shop "stuffed" with everything from snakes to baby elephants to zebras. Also on display are collections of butterflies, shells and minerals from all over the world. Kids seem to love this place. You have to go upstairs! The shop also sells planters, clothes and other household items (some modeled on the stuffed animals). Very quirky! It's closed on Sunday.

Head back toward the café and up rue de Bac in the opposite direction.

On this short block, you'll find everything from a butcher shop to a fish shop, and an attractive antique shop called **Magnolia**. Notice that horse head above one of the shops on your left? That means that the store still sells horse meat.

When you get to rue de Grenelle, make a left.

As you head down rue de Grenelle, you can stop at the **Musée Maillol (Fondation Dina Vierny-Musée Maillol)** at 61. The works of Aristide Maillol, a contemporary of Matisse, are here along with rare sketches by Picasso, Cézanne, Degas and other 20th-century artists. The museum also features important exhibits. It opens at 11 a.m. and is closed on Tuesdays.

Next to the museum is the **Fontaine des Quatre-Saisons**, completed in 1745. It's decorated with figures representing the four seasons (and a few cherubs thrown in for good measure).

You can't miss the cream-colored façade at number 51 of **Barthélemy**. This small, popular cheese shop is where Parisians come for their cheeses. The staff is extremely knowledgeable and helpful. You'll know when you're getting close as you can smell the shop as you approach. When you walk in, you're overtaken by the intense smell of some of the best cheeses available in France.

Let's backtrack to the café (down rue de Grenelle to rue du Bac). Turn right onto boulevard St-Germain-des-Prés. Walk down the left side of this famous boulevard.

At 218 is **Madeleine Gely**, a shop that's been making handmade umbrellas since 1834.

You have not experienced Paris unless you visit one of its many cafés. **Café de Flore** is at 172 boulevard St-Germain-des-Prés. Just a few steps away is **Café Les Deux Magots** at 6 place St-Germain-des-Prés.   Great people-watching at both of these famous cafés.

In between Café Les Deux Magots and Café de Flore is **La Hune**, at 170 boulevard St-Germain, This incredible bookstore is packed until midnight with Parisian and foreign "intellectuals." There's an extensive architecture and art section upstairs.

Take a left at place St-Germain-des-Prés.

Stop into the **Eglise St-Germain-des-Prés**. This church dates back to the 6th century. A Gothic choir, 19th-century spire and Romanesque paintings all attest to its long history.

As you exit the church, head right and then turn right onto rue de l'Abbaye.

On the right side of rue de l'Abbaye is the rose-colored 17th-century **Palais Abbatial**.

Take a left into place Fürstenberg.

At the center of **place Fürstenberg** is a white-globed lamppost. Look familiar? This scenic square has been seen in many films. It's often filled with street musicians, some of them surprisingly good.

Head back to rue de l'Abbaye and continue down the street which turns into rue de Bourbon-le-Château.

On the corner is a wonderful wine shop **La Dernière Goutte**.

Take a left on the attractive rue de Buci.

On rue de Buci, you'll pass along small cafés and interesting shops on a mostly pedestrian street. At the intersection of rue de Buci and rue St-André-des-Arts, you'll find lively cafés, interesting shops and a typical French outdoor market at certain times of the day.

Rue de Buci turns into rue St-André-des-Arts. Take a right at 61.

The **cour du Commerce** is a cobblestone alleyway off of la rue St-André-des-Arts, which is lined with wonderful shops and restaurants (including the historic **Procope**) to fit all pocketbooks.

At the end of the passageway, turn left and you'll be back on boulevard St-Germain. Continue on this street and take a right onto boulevard St-Michel.

On your left at the intersection is the **Musée de Cluny** (**Musée National du Moyen Age/ Thermes de Cluny**) at 6 place Paul-Painlevé. The building that houses this museum (the **Hôtel de Cluny**) has had many lives. It's been a Roman bathhouse in the 3rd century (you can still visit the ruins downstairs), a mansion for a religious abbot in the 15th century, a royal residence, and, since 1844, a museum. Don't miss the chapel on the second floor. It's a splendid example of flamboyant Gothic architecture. If you're interested in medieval arts and crafts, you must visit this museum. Chalices, manuscripts, crosses, vestments, carvings, sculptures and the acclaimed Lady and the Unicorn tapestries are all here. You enter through the cobblestoned **Court of Honor** (**Cour d'Honneur**) surrounded by the Gothic building with its gargoyles and turrets. Even if you don't visit the museum, you can visit the beautiful medieval garden.

Continue down the boulevard St-Michel.

On your left, you'll see the beautiful fountains in the **place de la Sorbonne**. This is the site of one of the most famous universities in the world. Take a break here at one of the many cafés and soak in the university ambience.

Return to boulevard St-Michel and continue in the same direction.

On your right, you'll soon see the black-and-gold fence surrounding the huge **Luxembourg Gardens**, where you'll end your walk. These formal French gardens are referred to as the heart of the Left Bank. Also here is the

Palais du Luxembourg (Luxembourg Palace), the home of the French Senate, and the **Musée du Luxembourg**, featuring temporary exhibitions of some of the big names in the history of art.

You can return to the intersection of boulevard St-Michel and boulevard St-Germain-des-Prés and take the Cluny-La Sorbonne métro back to your hotel.

MARAIS WALK

Walk C. See map on page 11. (Highlights: Musée Picasso, place des Vosges, and Centre Pompidou).

Take the métro to the St-Paul stop. When you get out of the métro, you'll be on rue St-Antoine.

Start walking (west) on the right side of rue St-Antoine until you reach 101, the **Eglise St-Paul-St-Louis**. Stop into this Baroque church with its huge dome dating back to the 1600s. Take a look at the Delacroix painting *Christ on the Mount of Olives* and the shell-shaped holy water fonts.

Continue on rue St-Antoine until you reach rue St-Paul. Turn right on rue St-Paul and then turn right at 23/25/27 rue St-Paul.

You're now in the **Village St-Paul**, an attractive passageway with interesting stores that is known for its antique shops.

Head back to the intersection of rue St-Paul and rue St-Antoine. Take a right, cross the street and walk to 62 rue St-Antoine.

Look at the exterior of the **Hôtel Sully**, a mansion in the French Renaissance style and the headquarters for administering France's historic monuments (**Caisse Nationale des Monuments Historiques**). Walk into the courtyard and beautiful garden.

Continue down rue St-Antoine and make a left at rue de Birague.

You'll now enter the **place des Vosges**, simply the most beautiful square in Paris, in France, and probably in all of Europe. It's the oldest square in Paris. It's a beautiful and quiet park surrounded by stone and red brick houses. Don't miss it! If you want, you can stop at **Victor Hugo's Home (Maison de Victor Hugo)**, 6 place des Vosges to view this 19th-century literary legend's home (he wrote *Les Miserables* and *The Hunchback of Notre Dame*).

Need a break? Stop in at **Ma Bourgogne**, 19 place des Vosges. This café/restaurant serves traditional Parisian cuisine and specializes in roast chicken. It's a great place for coffee.

After your break, it's back to rue St-Antoine. Take a left. At the end of rue St-Antoine is a huge traffic roundabout.

You're now at the **place de la Bastille**. The notorious Bastille prison was torn down over 200 years ago by mobs during the French Revolution. Today, it's a roundabout traffic circle where cars speed around the 170-foot **July Column**. On the opposite side is the modern **Opéra Bastille**.

This is another opportunity for a break as there are many cafés around the place de la Bastille.

> RESTAURANT TIP
> Café de L'Industrie
> *11th/Métro Bastille*
> *16 rue St-Sabin*
> *Phone: 01/47.00.13.53*
>
> Near the Opéra Bastille, this inexpensive café features a limited menu, a diverse wine list and an artsy crowd. Inexpensive.

On nearby rue Richard Lenoir (a street off the traffic circle, to your left as you're looking at the **July Column**), the outdoor **Marché Bastille** market is held every Thursday and Sunday. It's filled with colorful vendors selling everything from stinky cheese to African masks.

At the end of rue St-Antoine, turn left and walk a short distance and then turn left on rue de la Bastille.

At 5 rue de la Bastille is **Bofinger**, a beautiful glass-roofed *brasserie* with lots of stained glass and brass. It's the oldest Alsatian *brasserie* in Paris and still serves traditional dishes like *choucroute* (sauerkraut) and large platters of shellfish. Across the street and less expensive is **Le Petit Bofinger**.

Turn right from rue de la Bastille onto rue des Tournelles.

You'll pass another well-known restaurant at 38 rue des Tournelles. **Baracane** is an intimate, moderately priced restaurant featuring the specialties of Southwest France. Phone: 01/ 42.71.43.33, Closed Sat. (lunch) and Sun.

Turn left at rue du Pas-de-la-Mule.

At 6 rue du Pas-de-la-Mule you'll find the fascinating **Instruments Musicaux Anciens**. This curious little place, once a butcher shop, is jammed with musical instruments, from accordions to zithers. Stop in if it's open (most afternoons).

Continue down rue du Pas-de-la-Mule through the arcades of the place des Vosges. This street turns into the rue des Francs Bourgeois.

At the corner of rue des Francs Bourgeois and rue de Sévigné is the often-overlooked **Musée Carnavalet**. You'll find antiques, portraits and artifacts dating back to the late 1700s in this free museum. The section on the French Revolution with its guillotines is interesting as is the royal bedroom. There are exhibits across the courtyard at the **Hôtel le Peletier de St-Fargeau**. It's closed Mondays.

DETOUR

Off of rue des Francs Bourgeois, you can turn left down rue Pavée and then right onto rue des Rosiers and you find yourself in the heart of **Jewish Paris**. Rue des Rosiers is a great place to get a falafel sandwich and to view shop windows filled with Jewish artifacts. Stop at **Jo Goldenberg**, the famous Jewish deli at number 7. You'll need to retrace your steps back to rue des Francs Bourgeois. ❁

Continue on rue des Francs Bourgeois and make a right on rue Elzévir.

You'll pass the **Musée Cognacq-Jay** at 8 rue Elzévir. This free museum houses the 18th-century art and furniture collection of the founder of La Samaritaine department store. Works by Rembrandt, Fragonard, Boucher and others are here in this quiet museum located in the **Hôtel Donon**, an elegant mansion. It's closed Mondays.

Continue down rue Elzévir. It intersects with rue de Thorigny.

At 5 rue de Thorigny, you'll find the **Musée Picasso** (don't worry; if you're getting lost, there are signs directing you to the museum). This houses the world's largest collection of the works of Picasso in a 17th-century mansion. It's closed on Tuesdays.

Head back to rue des Francs Bourgeois.

At 60 rue des Francs Bourgeois, you'll find the **Musée de l'Histoire de France/Musée des Archives Nationales**. This museum has France's most famous documents including those written by Joan of Arc, Marie Antoinette and Napoleon. It's located in the **Hôtel de Clisson**, a palace dating back to 1371, the highlight of which is the incredibly ornate, oval-shaped **Salon Ovale**. It's closed Tuesdays.

Rue des Francs Bourgeois becomes rue Rambuteau. As you pass rue du Temple, you'll begin to see your final stop.

You can't miss the **Centre**

Georges Pompidou at place Georges-Pompidou. The building is a work of art in itself. The controversial building is "ekoskeletal" (the plumbing, elevators and ducts all are exposed and brightly painted). There's a great view from the rooftop restaurant (**Georges**). Don't miss the **Stravinsky Fountain** with its moving mobile sculptures and circus atmosphere just to the south of the museum. Notice the red pouty lips in the fountain!

After you've had enough of the museum, head right over to the **Café Beaubourg** facing the museum. It's crowded with an artsy crowd and recommended for a drink and perhaps a snack. The food is not that great, but the bathrooms are worth the trip.

You'll end your walk here and you can take the métro Rambuteau back to your hotel.

MAJOR SIGHTS WALK
Walk D. See map on pages 46-47.
(Highlights: Eiffel Tower, Bateaux Mouches, Arc de Triomphe, and Champs-Élysées).
Take the métro to Ecole Militaire.

At the métro stop, you'll see the huge **Ecole Militaire** (it's open only on special occasions). This Royal Military Academy was built in the mid-1700s to edu-cate the sons of military officers. The building is a grand example of the French Classical style with its dome and Corinthian pillars. Its most famous alumnus was Napoleon.

Now start walking toward the Eiffel Tower.

The **Champ de Mars** are the long gardens that stretch from the **Ecole Militaire** to the **Eiffel Tower**.

It's time to visit one of the most well-known landmarks in the world. It's best to visit the **Eiffel Tower** in either early morning or late evening when the crowds are smaller. Created for the 1889 Universal Exhibition, the Eiffel Tower was built by the same man who designed the framework for the Statue of Liberty. At first it was called, among other things, an "iron monster" when it was erected. Gustave-Alexandre Eiffel never meant for his 7,000-ton tower to be permanent and it was almost torn down in 1909. Today, it's without a doubt the most recognizable structure in the world. Well over 200 million people have visited this monument. You can either take the elevator to one of three landings or climb the 1,652 stairs.

Walk behind the Eiffel Tower and cross the bridge (the Pont d'Iéna).

Once you cross the bridge, you'll be in the **Trocadéro Gardens (Jardins du Trocadéro)**, home to the **Palais de Chaillot**. This huge palace, surrounded by more than 60 fountains, was built 60 years ago and is home to several museums.

After taking in the gardens and palace, turn right (as you face the palace and gardens) on the avenue de New York along the Seine River.

While you're on the avenue de New York, on the left, you'll see the **Palais de Tokyo**, a contemporary art center (and one of the most glamorous places for skateboarders).

Follow avenue de New York until you reach the Pont de l'Alma (the second bridge).

This bridge, the **Pont de l'Alma**, was created in the time of Napoleon III. The original bridge was replaced in 1972 with the present-day steel structure. Take a look at one of the fanciest high-water markers in the world. Originally, there were four Second Empire soldier statues that decorated the old bridge. Only one, Zouave, remains below the bridge. Parisians use it to measure the height of the water in the Seine. It's said that in 1910, the water reached all the way to Zouave's chin.

You're now at the **place de l'Alma**, one of the most luxurious areas in Paris.

If you have never been in Paris (or for that matter, even if you have), you might want to take a tour of the Seine on the **Bateaux Mouches**. These boats depart from the Right Bank next to the place de l'Alma.

At the place de l'Alma, you'll see a replica of the torch of the Statue of Liberty.

The replica of the torch of the Statue of Liberty was erected here in 1987. It was meant to commemorate the French Resistance during World War II. It just happens to be over the tunnel where Princess Diana and her boyfriend Dodi Al-Fayedh were killed in an automobile crash in 1997. The **Liberty Flame** is now an unofficial shrine covered with notes, flowers and prayers to the dead princess.

Head down the avenue Marceau. It's one of the streets off of place de l'Alma. It's about a 10-minute walk on avenue Marceau to the Arc de Triomphe.

When you get to the **Arc de Triomphe**, don't try to walk across the square. This is Paris's busiest intersection. Twelve avenues pour into the circle around the Arc. There are underground passages, however, that take you to the Arc. There's an observation deck providing one of the greatest views of Paris. There's no cost to visit the Arc but there's an admission fee for the exhibit of photos of the Arc throughout history and for the observation deck. If you aren't impressed by the view down the Champs-Élysées, you really shouldn't have come to Paris.

If you've had enough walking, here's a good place to take the métro back to your hotel. But if you want to continue, head down the Champs-Élysées.

The left side of the **Champs-Élysées** has more interesting retail shops rather than the banks and businesses on the right side. This street is one of the most famous streets in the world. It's home to expensive retail shops, fast-food chains, car dealers, banks, huge movie theatres and overpriced cafés. Despite this, you can sit at a café and experience great people-watching (mostly tourists).

One interesting shop is the large **Sephora Perfume Store** at 74 Champs-Élysées (open daily until midnight). The large "wheel of scents" lets you smell scents from chocolate to flower to wood!

On the left side, toward the end of the Champs-Élysées (at number 10) is **Le Pavillon Élysée**, an elegant oblong glass building built for the 1900 World's Fair. It's home to **Lenôtre**, a café, kitchen shop and cooking school all in one. Lenôtre's specialty is its desserts, and you can enjoy one with a cup of delicious coffee on the lovely stone terrace that looks onto the gardens.

At avenue Winston-Churchill you can gaze at the recently renovated **Grande** and **Petit Palais**, both built for the 1900 World Exhibition and, like the Eiffel Tower, never meant to be permanent structures. These magnificent buildings remain today in all their glory.

Continue down the Champs-Élysées until you reach the huge place de la Concorde.

At the end of your walk, admire the huge **place de la Concorde**. In the center of this 21 acres stands the **Obélisque de Louxor (Obelisk of Luxor)**, an Egyptian column from the 13th century and covered with hieroglyphics. It was moved here in 1833. Now a traffic roundabout, it was here that Louis XVI and Marie Antoinette were guillotined during the French Revolution.

You can take the Métro Concorde back to your hotel. The métro stop is at the far left side of the place de la Concorde.

The **Concorde métro** stop has 44,000 blue-and-white lettered ceramic tiles on its walls. Don't read French? I always wondered if they meant anything. In fact, they do. They spell out the seventeen articles of the declaration of the *Rights of Man and the Citizens* that the National Assembly adopted in 1789.

MONTMARTRE WALK
Walk E. See map on page 83. (Highlights: Sacré-Coeur, Espace Salvador Dali, and Moulin Rouge). Note: There are lots of steps and steep, cobbled streets on this walk.

Your walk begins at the Abbesses métro stop.

This métro stop is the deepest in Paris and stands on the site of a medieval abbey. You'll know this right away as there are tons of stairs to climb just to get out of the métro. You can also take an elevator to the top.

When you get out of the métro, you'll be at the **place des Abbesses**. Take in the picturesque triangular "square" which features one of the few remaining curvy, green wrought-iron Art Nouveau entrances.

Off of the place des Abbesses, take rue Yvonne-Le-Tac which becomes rue Tardieu.

You'll be at the base of the **Basilique du Sacré-Coeur (Sacred Heart Basilica)**. It's at the top of the hill (*butte*) and dominates this neighborhood. You can't miss the Basilica with its white onion domes and Byzantine and Romanesque architecture. Completed in 1919, it's named for Christ's sacred heart which some believe is in the crypt. Inside, you'll find gold mosaics, but the real treat is the view of Paris from the dome.

*You now have three ways to get to the Basilica. For the price of a métro ticket, you can take the funicular (cable car). You can also take the 224 steps up **rue Foyatier** (to the left of the cable car), one of*

> **DETOUR**
> If you need a break after visiting the Basilica, you can stop at the interesting and picturesque **Café L'Été en Pente Douce** (which means "summer on a gentle slope") at 23 rue Muller. If you're facing the Basilica, take the steps down to your right (rue Maurice-Utrillo) and at the bottom is rue Muller and the café. ❖

the most photographed sights in Paris, or you can take the steps directly in front of the Basilica.

With the Basilica to your back, turn to the right and follow rue Azaïs and then take a right onto rue St-Eleuthère.

On your right will be the **Eglise St-Pierre**, one of the oldest churches in Paris. The Roman marble columns date back to the 1100s.

Head down rue Norvins (it's to your left with the Eglise St-Pierre to your back) through the place du Tertre.

The attractive **place du Tertre** is overrun with tourists and artists trying to paint your portrait. There's a circus-like atmosphere here.

Across the square is the short rue du Calvaire. Turn right into the place du Calvaire (right before you reach the stairs heading down the hill).

On the other side of this attractive square is our next stop, **Espace Salvador-Dali**, at 11 rue Poulbot. Black walls, weird music with Dali's voice and dim lighting all make this museum of the works of Salvador Dali an interesting experience. Come here if you're a fan of his work to

see 300 lithographs and etchings and 25 sculptures.

Continue on rue Poulbot, make a left on rue Norvins and a quick right down rue des Saules.

DETOUR

If you take a right onto beautiful rue Cortot, you can visit the **Musée du Vieux Montmartre** at 12 rue Cortot. Renoir and van Gogh are just a few of the artists who have occupied this 17th-century house. It now has a collection of mementos of the neighborhood, including paintings, posters and photographs. ✳

Continue down rue des Saules.

On your right is the last remaining **vineyard** in Paris at the corner of rue St-Vincent and rue des Saules near the place Jules Joffrin. They still sell wine here. The labels are designed by local artists. The harvesting of the grapes in October gives the residents of Montmartre yet another excuse to have a festival.

You'll likely hear French folk tunes coming out of the shuttered cottage at the picturesque intersection of rue des Saules and rue St-Vincent. **Au Lapin Agile/Cabaret des Assassins** was once frequented by Picasso. Today, you'll sit at small wooden tables and listen to *chansonniers* (singers). A truly Parisian experience.

DETOUR

If you're interested in ancient and modern Jewish art, you can continue down the many stairs of rue des Saules to the **Musée d'Art Juif** at 42 rue des Saules. It's closed. Fri., Sat. and Aug.

Turn left on rue St-Vincent and make a left at place Constantine Pecquer. Climb the stairs (yes, more stairs!). At the top is rue Girardon.

The park on your right is **Square Suzanne Buisson**, named after a leader of the French Resistance. According to legend, St-Denis (after being decapitated) carried his head here and washed it in the fountain. There's a statue of him holding his head.

Follow rue Girardon until you reach the corner of rue Lepic.

In the 19th century, Montmartre had many vineyards and over 40 windmills. One of the two surviving windmills, the **Moulin de la Galette**, is on this corner. If it looks familiar, it's the windmill depicted by Renoir in his painting of the same name. It's now part of a restaurant.

From here turn right on rue Lepic.

You'll see the other surviving **windmill** on your right at the corner of rue Tholozé.

Continue downhill (finally!) on rue Lepic.

You may want to have a glass of wine at **O'Vinéa**, a wine bar at 69 rue Lepic.

Van Gogh lived at 54 rue Lepic in 1886.

The movie *Amélie*'s lead character is a waitress. Visit Amélie's 1950s bistro **Bar-tabac des Deux Moulins** at 15 rue Lepic. You'll run into a few tourists and mostly locals enjoying good homemade desserts and standard bistro fare.

At the end of rue Lepic at place Blanche, turn right onto boulevard de Clichy.

You'll see the **Moulin Rouge**, at 82 boulevard de Clichy. Originally a red windmill, this dance hall has been around since 1889. It's without a doubt the most famous cabaret in the world. Toulouse-Lautrec memorialized the Moulin Rouge in his paintings, and it got a boost in business from the more recent movie of the same name. Looking for a little bit of Vegas? You'll find it here.

Here, you can head home at the métro Blanche stop (especially if you have kids with you) or you can head left (with the Moulin Rouge to your back) down boulevard de Clichy to place Pigalle.

You come to **place Pigalle** for only one thing: sex. Littered with sex shops, this area was known as "Pig Alley" during World War II.

You can end your trip here at the métro Pigalle stop.

CULINARY WALKS

Paris is the food capital of the world. If you're interested in food, Paris offers everything you ever wanted. If nothing else, food markets are very interesting. Though you may feel intimidated by the wild goings-on (not to mention the sights and smells), it's absolutely worth a trip to see a real outdoor Parisian market. Filled with colorful vendors, stinky cheese, fresh produce, poultry and hanging rabbits, this is Paris at its most real, diverse and beautiful. Parisians still shop (some every day) at food markets around the city. Unless

noted otherwise, all are open Tuesday through noon on Sunday. Some of the best-known are:

- **Rue Montorgueil** (1st/Métro Les Halles)
- **Rue Mouffetard** (5th/Métro Censier-Daubenton)
- **Rue de Buci** (6th/Métro Mabillon)
- **Rue Cler** (7th/Métro École Militaire)
- **Marché Bastille** on the **boulevard Richard Lenoir** (11th/Métro Bastille) (open Thursday and Sunday)
- **Rue Daguerre** (14th/Métro Denfert-Rochereau) and
- **Rue Poncelet** (17th/Métro Ternes).

Markets are places you might appreciate as you would a museum, but there are other places around Paris where you can also see and experience food in a unique setting. In addition to food markets and specialty shops, there are several areas in Paris where many restaurants are concentrated in small pockets. These are areas that are charming just in and of themselves, nice to walk through and nice to eat in, particularly outside in good weather.

One area is on rue Pot-de-Fer between la rue Tournefort and la rue Mouffetard, just off the market. It's a slip of a street but it's lined with charming restaurants with clothed tables set for dinner, colored lights hanging from the roof overhangs, and a uniquely Parisian ambiance (Métro Monge).

Uniquely Parisian is not the Passage Brady in the 10th arrondissement. You can enter the narrow passage around 33 boulevard de Strasbourg and find mostly Indian, but also Turkish and Moroccan, restaurants in an interestingly Indian setting. These are inexpensive restaurants in a working-class neighborhood, and the passage, while exotic in many ways, is not upscale (Métro Château d'Eau).

There are several restaurants and bars on the lovely place Ste-Catherine (between la rue Malher and la rue de Sévigné) in the Marais, 4th. There are many restaurants in this neighborhood in general, but the place Ste-Catherine is a special, quiet respite in this newly fashionable area (Métro St-Paul).

You'll find loads of restaurants off of la rue St-Jacques in the area around la rue St-Séverin and la rue de la Huchette in the 5th. This area, a short walk from Notre-Dame, is filled with French, Italian, Greek and other restaurants jammed into small streets. It's a very pleasant walk, and you're bound to find somewhere to eat. Nearby in the 6th is the cour du Commerce, a tiny alleyway off of la rue St-André-des-Arts, which is lined with restaurants to fit all pocketbooks (Métros St-Michel, Odéon or Cluny-La Sorbonne).

3. MISCELLANY

TIPS ON BUDGET DINING

There's no need to spend a lot of money in Paris to have good food. Of course it helps when the euro is weaker than the dollar, but there are all kinds of fabulous foods to be had inexpensively all over Paris.

Eat at a neighborhood restaurant or bistro. The menu, with prices, is posted in the window. Never order anything whose price is not known in advance. If you see *selon grosseur* (sometimes abbreviated as s/g), this means that you're paying by weight, which can be extremely expensive. Avoid restaurants and bistros with English menus.

Delis and food stores can provide cheap and wonderful meals. Buy some cheese, bread, wine and other snacks and have a picnic in one of Paris's great parks.

Lunch, even at the most expensive restaurants listed in this guide, always has a lower fixed price. So, have lunch as your main meal.

Large department stores frequently have supermarkets (in the basement) and restaurants that have reasonably priced food. La Samaritaine (1st/Métro Pont Neuf, 19 rue de la Monnaie) has a supermarket and a reasonably priced café on the 10th floor.

Street vendors generally sell inexpensive and terrific food.

For the cost of a cup of coffee or a drink, you can linger at a café and watch the world pass you by for as long as you want.

Kids seem to love Hippopotamus, a chain of inexpensive restaurants with over twenty locations in Paris.

PARIS BY THE MONTH

January: If you love shopping, it's time for post-holiday bargains. Parisians call it "*les soldes.*" Paris is also host to the international ready-to-wear fashion shows held at the Parc des Expositions (15th).

February: Events highlight France's important agricultural industry with the *Salon de l'Agriculture*. Included in the celebration are food and wine from throughout France.

March: At the end of the month is the *Foire du Trône*, a huge amusement park held at the Bois de Vincennes (12th). With Ferris wheels, circus attractions and carousels, it's like a sophisticated county fair.

April: Paris is home to the International Marathon. On the first weekend, spectators line the Champs-Elysées to watch the women's and men's marathons. Some of the best jazz artists come to Paris at the end of the month for the *Fête de Jazz*. Events and concerts featuring jazz artists are held throughout the city.

May: Tennis is king in late May as Paris hosts the French Open (they call it "*Roland Garros*").

June: Music fills the air during the many concerts as part of the *Fête de la Musique*. From Guatemalan street musicians to serious opera, you'll be exposed to Paris's diversity. Most concerts are free.

July: In early July, Paris hosts a huge gay pride parade. On the 14th, Parisians celebrate *Le Quatorze Juillet* or Bastille Day with city-wide celebrations, fireworks and a huge military parade down the Champs-Élysées. In late July, the Tour de France is completed when bikers ride down the Champs-Élysées. This is also a huge month for *soldes* (clothing sales).

August: Sunbathe, drink and celebrate the Seine River at *Paris-Plage*. Hundreds of deck chairs, umbrellas, cabanas and even palm trees are all brought to the Right Bank of the river from Pont de Sully to Pont Neuf. You can enjoy the sun, have a drink or two and a snack. No, I don't recommend that you swim in the Seine. In the evening, musicians play along the river.

September: You can visit historical monuments (some of which are usually closed to the public) during *Fête du Patrimoine*. In late September, Paris again hosts the international ready-to-wear fashion convention at Parc des Expositions (15th).

October: Thousands of horse-racing fans arrive in Paris for the *Prix de l'Arc de Triomphe Lucien Barriere*. It's considered to be the ultimate thoroughbred horse race. It's held at the Hippodrome de Longchamps. (16th).

November: Only in France would the arrival of wine be celebrated as a huge event. Get ready to drink Beaujolais Nouveau (a fruity wine from Burgundy) on the third Thursday.

December: A skating rink is installed in front of the Hôtel de Ville (City Hall). The large windows of the major department stores (Bon Marché, BHV, Galeries Lafayette, La Samaritaine and Printemps) are decorated in interesting (sometimes bizarre) Christmas themes. One of the best ways to experience Christmas in Paris is to walk down one of the following areas decorated with beautiful lights: Avenue des Champs-Élysées, Rue du Faubourg-St-Honoré, Rue de Castiglione, Quartier Montmartre, place des Victoires, place Vendôme, Avenue Montaigne, Rue Montorgueil, Rue des Petits-Carreaux and Rue de la Paix. Fête de St-Sylvestre (New Year's Eve) is celebrated throughout the city. At midnight, the Eiffel Tower is a virtual light show and the city is filled with champagne-drinking Parisians welcoming the new year and a few tourists hoping they'll return to this great city in the new year.

THE BRIDGES OF PARIS

There are 36 bridges over the Seine that don't just connect one bank with the other. They should be considered monuments in and of themselves. They are places for strolling, for stopping to kiss someone you love, for viewing the beauty of Paris and pondering life.

Here are a few of the most famous:

Pont Alexandre III

Built for the World Fair of 1900, this elegant steel bridge has one arch, winged horses, cherubs and ornate lamps. It's named after Alexander III, the father of Nicholas II of Russia, who laid the foundation stone. It has a wonderful view of Les Invalides. (Métro Invalides)

Pont Neuf

The twelve arches of the Pont Nuef connect the Ile de la Cité with both banks of the Seine River. Construction of this bridge began in 1578 and was completed in 1604. Despite its name (which means "new bridge"), it's the oldest bridge in Paris. Pause here for a view of the Louvre Museum on the Right Bank and the beautiful apartments on the Left Bank. (Métro Pont Neuf)

Pont des Arts

This bridge, at the tip of the Ile de la Cité, dates back to 1803 and was the first pedestrian-only bridge in Paris. It has a fantastic view of the Pont Neuf, the Louvre and Notre-Dame. (Métro Louvre)

Pont St-Louis

This pedestrian-only metal

arched bridge is relatively new (1970), and connects the Ile de la Cité and Ile St-Louis. It has great views of Notre-Dame and the Hôtel de Ville (City Hall). There almost always is a street band (usually playing jazz) on the bridge. (Métro Cité)

Pont Royal

It's one of the oldest bridges in Paris and has a great view of the Louvre. (Métro Tuileries)

Pont Solférino

This double-decker bridge spans the Seine between the Pont Royal and the Pont de la Concorde, near the Musée d'Orsay. It's located at one of the most beautiful spots along the Seine. (Métro Solférino)

Pont de Sully

This bridge dates back to 1874 and is actually two independent steel bridges that extend from the Ile St-Louis to either side of the river. Great views of Notre-Dame, Ile St-Louis and Ile de la Cité. (Métro Sully Morland)

Pont de la Concorde

The stones from the burned Bastille were used to build this bridge that connects the place de la Concorde on the Right Bank and the Palais Bourbon on the Left Bank. (Métro Concorde)

Pont Charles-de-Gaulle

This new metal bridge built in 1993 is in the shape of an airplane wing, and links the quai de la Rapée (12th) and the quai d'Austerlitz (13th). Depite its interesting design concept, it's not particularly popular among Parisians. (Métro Gare d'Austerlitz)

Pont Mirabeau

Built in 1893, this beautiful steel bridge has been the subject of poetry (by Apollinaire) and pop songs (the Pogues). (Métro Mirabeau).

RESOURCES

Airports/Arrival

Paris has two international airports: Charles de Gaulle (Roissy) and Orly. An Air France shuttle operates between the airports every 30 minutes. The trip takes up to 75 minutes and costs 12€.

At Charles de Gaulle, a free shuttle bus connects Aérogare 1 (used by most foreign carriers) with Aérogare 2 (used primarily by Air France). This bus also drops you off at the Roissy train station. Line B departs every 15 minutes from 5 a.m. to midnight to major métro stations. The cost is 8€ (13€ for first-class). Connecting métro lines will take you to your final destination.

A taxi ride costs about 40€ to the city center. The price will be a bit higher than on the meter as a charge will be added for your baggage. At night, fares are up to

50% higher. You'll find the taxi line outside the terminals. It will frequently be long, but moves quite fast. Never take an unmetered taxi!

Orly has two terminals: Sud (south) for international flights, and Ouest (west) for domestic flights. A free shuttle bus connects the two. A taxi from Orly to the city costs about 35€ and up to 50% more at night.

Orly Val is a monorail (stopping at both terminals) to the RER train station at Anthony (a ten-minute ride), then on to the city on the RER (Line B) train. The ride takes 30 minutes. The cost is 9€ for both the monorail and the train ride.

Cars
Are you crazy? Parking is chaotic, gas is extremely expensive, and driving in Paris is an unpleasant "adventure." With the incredible public transportation system in Paris, there's absolutely no reason to rent a car.

Children
An excellent source for stuff to do with kids is Open Road's *Paris With Kids*.

Customs
Citizens of the US who have been away more than 48 hours can bring home $800 of merchandise duty-free every 30 days.

For more information, go to Traveler Information ("Know Before You Go") at www.customs.gov. Canadians can bring back C$750 each year if you have been gone for 7 days or more.

Dogs
Parisians really love their dogs. In restaurants, it's not uncommon to find several dogs under tables, or even on their own chairs.

Eating
The bill in a restaurant is called *l'addition*...but the bill in a bar is called *le compte* or *la note*; confusing? It's easier if you just make a scribbling motion with your fingers on the palm of your hand.

A service charge is almost always added to your bill. Depending on the service, it's sometimes appropriate to leave an additional 5 to 10%. The menu will usually note that service is included (*service compris*). Sometimes this is abbreviated with the letters s.c. The letters s.n.c. stand for *service non compris*; this means that the service is not included in the price, and you must leave a tip. You'll sometimes find *couvert* or cover charge on your menu (a small charge just for placing your butt at the table).

And don't forget to bring my *Eating & Drinking in Paris*!

A menu is a fixed-price meal, not that piece of paper listing the food items. If you want what we consider a menu, you need to ask for *la carte*. The menu is almost always posted on the front of the restaurant so you know what you're getting into, both foodwise and pricewise, before you enter.

RESTAURANT PRICES
Restaurant prices in this book are for a main course and without wine:

Inexpensive: under $10
Moderate: $11-$20
Expensive: $21-$30
Very Expensive: over $30. �֍

Electricity

The electrical current in Paris is 220 volts as opposed to 110 volts found at home. Don't fry your electric razor, hairdryer or laptop. You'll need a converter and an adapter. Some laptops don't require a converter, but why are you bringing that anyway?

Embassies

Canada: 8th/Métro Franklin-D. Roosevelt, 35 avenue Montaigne, Phone: 01/44.43.29.00
US: 1st/Métro Concorde, 2 rue St-Florentin, Phone: 01/43.12.22.22 or 01/43.12.23.47

E-Mail

Cyber cafés seem to pop up everywhere (and go out of business quickly). You shouldn't have difficulty finding a place to e-mail home. Remember that French keyboards are different than those found in the USA and Canada. The going rate is about 2€ per hour.

Flying Times

Flight times from major cities are:
From LA: 11 hours
From Chicago: 9 hours
From New York: 7 hours
From Atlanta: 8 hours
From London: 1 hour
From Sydney: 21.5 hours

Holidays

New Year's: January 1
Easter
Ascension (40 days after Easter)
Pentecost (seventh Sunday after Easter)
May Day: May 1
Victory in Europe: May 8
Bastille Day: July 14
Assumption of the Virgin Mary: August 15
All Saints': November 1
Armistice: November 11
Christmas: December 25

Insurance

Check with your health-care provider. Some policies don't cover you oversees. If that's the case, you may want to obtain medical insurance (one such provider is

HOTELS
Prices for a Double Room

Expensive (over $200)

Ritz
1ˢᵗ/Métro Opéra
15 place Vendôme
Phone: 01/43.16.30.30
(800/223-6800)

George V (Four Seasons)
8ᵗʰ/Métro George V
31 avenue George V
Phone: 01/49.52.70.00
(800/332-3442)

Hôtel de l'Académie
7ᵗʰ/Métro St-Germain-des-Prés
32 rue des Sts-Pères
Phone: 01/45.49.80.00
(800/246-0041)

Jeu de Paume
4ᵗʰ/Métro Pont Marie
54 rue St-Louis-en-l'Ile
Phone: 01/43.26.14.18

Moderate ($125-$200)

Galileo
8ᵗʰ/Métro George V
54 rue Galilée
Phone: 01/47.20.66.06

Jardins du Luxembourg
5ᵗʰ/Métro Cluny-La Sorbonne
5 impasse Royer-Collard
Phone: 01/40.46.08.88

Grand Hôtel Malher
4ᵗʰ/Métro St-Paul
5 rue Malher
Phone: 01/42.72.60.92

Hôtel d'Orsay
7ᵗʰ/Métro Solférino
93 rue de Lille
Phone: 01/47.05.85.54

Inexpensive (under $125)

Hôtel du Champ de Mars
7ᵗʰ/Métro École Militaire
7 rue du Champ de Mars
Phone: 01/45.51.52.30

Saintonge
3ʳᵈ/Métro République
16 rue Saintonge
Phone: 01/42.77.91.13

Ermitage
18ᵗʰ/Métro Lamarck-Caulaincourt
24 rue Lamarck
Phone: 01/42.64.79.22

Grand Hôtel Jeanne d'Arc
4ᵗʰ/Métro St-Paul
3 rue Jarente
Phone: 01/48.87.62.11

found at www.medexassist.com). Given the uncertainties in today's world, you may also want to purchase trip-cancellation insurance (try www.travelguard.com). Make sure that your policy covers sickness, disasters, bankruptcy and State Department travel restrictions and warnings. In other words, read the fine print!

Language

Please, make the effort to speak a little French. It will get you a long way. Even if all you can say is *Parlez-vouz anglais?* (par-lay voo ahn-glay): Do you speak English? Gone are the days when Parisians were only interested in correcting your French.

Mealtimes

In Paris, lunch is served from noon to around 2 p.m., and dinner from 8 p.m. to 11 p.m. Restaurants usually have two seatings: at 8 or 8:30 p.m., and at 10 or 10:30 p.m. The restaurant will be less crowded and less smoky at the early seating. Make reservations!

Métro (Subway)

The métro system is clearly the best way to get around Paris. It's orderly, inexpensive and for the most part safe. You're rarely far from a métro station in Paris. They are marked by a yellow "M" in a circle or by those incredibly beautiful art nouveau archways with "Métropolitain" on them. Although you may be confused

when you first look at a métro map, if you simply follow the line that your stop is on and note the last stop (the last stop appears on all the signs), you'll soon be scurrying about underground like a Parisian. Service starts at 5:30 a.m. and ends between midnight and 1 a.m. Métro tickets are also valid on the RER and buses. Each ticket costs 1.30€. Buy a *carnet* (10 tickets for about 10€).

If you're staying in Paris for a longer period of time, a *carte orange* for zones 1 and 2 (Paris and nearby suburbs) costs about 15€ a week or about 45€ per month and allows unlimited use of both the métro and the bus system. You'll need a pass (you can get them at any major métro station) and a passport-size photo. That's why there are so many of those photo booths at stations. There are many options available for métro passes. Check them out.

> **KEEP YOUR TICKET!**
> Keep your ticket throughout your trip. An inspector can fine you if you can't produce a stamped ticket. ❖

Money

The euro (€) is the currency of France and most of Europe. Before you leave for Paris, it's a good idea to get some euros. It makes your arrival a lot easier. Call your credit-card company or bank before you leave to tell them that you'll be using your ATM or credit card outside the country. Many have automatic controls that can "freeze" your account if the computer program determines that there are charges outside your normal area. ATMs (of course, with fees) are the easiest way to change money in Paris. You'll find them everywhere. You can still get traveler's checks, but why bother?

Packing

Never pack prescription drugs, eyeglasses or valuables. Carry them on. Think black. It always works for men and women. Oh, and by the way, pack light. Don't ruin your trip by having to lug around huge suitcases.

Before you leave home, make copies of your passport, airline tickets and confirmation of hotel reservations. You should also make a list of your credit-card numbers and the telephone numbers for your credit-card companies. If you lose any of them (or they are stolen), you can call someone at home and have them provide the information to you. You should also pack copies of these documents separate from the originals.

Passports

You'll need a valid passport to enter France. If you're staying more than 90 days, you must obtain a visa. Canadians don't need visas.

Rest Rooms

There aren't a lot of public rest rooms. If you need to go, your best bet is to head (no pun intended) to the nearest café or brasserie. It's considered good manners to purchase something if you use the rest room. Some métro stations have public rest rooms. Another option are those strange self-cleaning rest rooms that look like some sort of pod found on some streets in Paris. Don't be shocked to walk into a rest room and find two porcelain footprints and a hole in the floor. These old "Turkish toilets" still exist. Hope you have strong thighs!

Shopping

Throughout this guide, you'll find recommended places to shop. The Parisians head to Monoprix, a supermarket and discount department store. There are locations throughout Paris. The stores are particularly known for their budget-priced, quality cosmetics.

Safety

Paris is one of the safest large cities in the world. Still, don't wear a "fanny pack;" it's a sign that you're a tourist and an easy target (especially in crowded tourist areas and the métro). Avoid wearing expensive jewelry in the métro.

Summer in Paris

In August, many restaurants and shops close for the month.

Taxes

Hotel and restaurant prices are required by law to include taxes and service charges. Value Added Tax (VAT or TVA in France) is nearly 20% (33% on luxury goods). The VAT is included in the price of goods (except services such as restaurants). Foreigners are entitled to a refund and must fill out a refund form. When you make your purchase, you should ask for the form and instructions if you're purchasing 182€ or more in one place and in one day (no combining). Yes, it can be a hassle.

Telephone

The country code for France is 33. The area code for Paris is 01. Calls beginning with 0800 are toll-free. To call Paris from the US you'll dial 011-33-1-plus the telephone number. You drop the 0 in the area code. To dial the US or Canada from Paris, dial 00 (wait for the tone) then dial 1 plus the area code and number. Phone cards are the cheapest way to call. Get one from many *tabacs*, métro stations or magazine kiosks. US-issued calling cards are terribly expensive to use from France.

Time

When it's noon in New York City, it's 6 p.m. in Paris. For hours of events or schedules, the French use the 24-hour clock. So 6 a.m. is 06h00 and 1 p.m. is 13h00.

Tipping

See the Eating section for tipping in restaurants. Other tips: 10% for taxi drivers, 1€ for room service, 1.50€ per bag to the hotel porter, 1.50€ per day for maid service and .50€ to bathroom attendants.

Water

Tap water is safe in Paris. Occasionally, you'll find *non potable* signs in rest rooms. This means that the water is not safe for drinking.

Web Sites

• Paris Tourist Office www.paris.org
• French Government Tourist Office www.franceguide.com
• US State Department Foreign Entry Requirements http://travel.state.gov/foreignentryreqs.html

Weather

Paris has an average temperature of 53 degrees F (35 degrees C). The horrific heat wave that struck in the summer of 2003 was unusual.

HELPFUL PHRASES

please, *s'il vous plait*
thank you, *merci*
yes, *oui*
no, *non*
good morning, *bonjour*
good afternoon, *bonjour*
good evening, *bonsoir*
good night (only when going to bed), *bonne nuit*
goodbye, *au revoir*
sorry, *désolé*
Do you speak English?, *parlez-vous anglais?*
I don't speak French, *je ne parle pas français*
excuse me, *pardon*
I don't understand, *je ne comprends pas*

I'd like a table, *je voudrais une table*
I'd like to reserve a table, *je voudrais réserver une table*
for one person, *pour une personne*
for two, *pour deux*
trois (3), *quatre* (4), *cinq* (5), *six* (6), *sept* (7), *huit* (8), *neuf* (9), *dix* (10) *personnes*
closed, *fermé*
Monday, *Lundi*
Tuesday, *Mardi*
Wednesday, *Mercredi*
Thursday, *Jeudi*
Friday, *Vendredi*
Saturday, *Samedi*
Sunday, *dimanche*

INDEX

Académie Français 39
African art 65
Airports/Arrival 116
amusement park 66
Ancien Cloître Quartier 12
antiques 30, 51, 99, 102
Aquaboulevard 81
Aquarium 74
Arab World Institute 36
Arc de Triomphe 53, 107
Arc du Carrousel 20
architecture 63
Arènes de Lutèce 36
Arrondissement 8, 14
art galleries 72
Asian art 63, 65
Assemblée Nationale 49
auctions 68
bakery 23

bars 26, 56, 61, 76
Bastille 72, 103
Bateau-Lavoir 85
Bateaux-Mouches 61, 106
Beaujolais Nouveau 115
Bibliothèque Nationale 75
bird market 10, 96
boat tour 61, 70, 106
Bois de Boulogne 66
Bois de Vincennes 75
bookstores 34, 44, 98, 100
Bourse (stock exchange) 17
Bourse du Commerce 22
Bouquinistes, Les 9
boutiques (designer/luxury) ... 62
bridges 115, 116
budget dining 113
Caisse Nationale des Monuments Historiques 30, 102

Canal St-Martin 70
candy/chocolates57, 60, 68, 72, 87
Carrousel du Louvre, Le 20
Catacombes, Les 77
cemeteries
    de Montmartre 86
    du Montparnasse 77
    du Passy 63
    du Père-Lachaise 89
    Dog Cemetery 91
Centre Nat. de la Photographie60
champagne bar 63
Champs-de-Mars 45, 105
Champs-Élysées 54, 107
Chantilly 93
Chartres 92
Château de Vincennes 75
cheese shops 50, 81, 100
children 113, 117
Chinatown 76
Chinese Pagoda 58
Chopin, Salle 13
christmas 24, 115
churches
    American Cathedral 61
    Basilique de St-Denis 90
    Basilique Ste-Clotilde 50
    Cathédrale Notre-Dame de
       Chartres 92
    Chapel of Our Lady of the
       Miraculous Medal 51
    Chapel of the Priests of the
       Congregation 52
    Dôme, Eglise du 48
    Madeleine, Eglise de la 58
    Notre-Dame 10, 12, 96
    St-Vincent de Paul 71
    St-Alexandre Nevsky 57
    Ste-Chapelle 9, 96
    St-Etienne-du-Mont 38
    St-Eustache 22
    St-Germain-des-Prés 44, 100
    St-Germain-l'Auxerrois 21
    St-Gervais-St-Protais 24
    St-Julien-le-Pauvre 34
    St-Merri 26
    St-Paul-St-Louis 30, 102
    St-Pierre 84, 109
    St-Roch 16
    St-Séverin 34

St-Sulpice 40
Sacred Heart Basilica
    (Sacré-Coeur) 82, 108
Cité de la Musique 88
City of Science and Industry .. 88
City Hall 23
concerts 10, 12, 34
cooking classes 27, 55
cour du Commerce 41, 101
Crypte Archéologique 10
crystal 64, 71
culinary walks 27, 111
customs 117
Défense, La 91
department stores 52, 66, 95
Deportation Memorial 13, 97
Deyrolle 50, 99
Disneyland Paris 92
dogs 117
driving 117
Drouot-Richelieu Auctions 68
eating 113, 117, 118
École Militaire 45, 105
Eiffel Tower (Tour Eiffel)45, 105
electricity 118
E-Mail 118
embassies 118
European Photography Center 30
Eurostar 70
fashion shows 113, 114
Fête de la Musique 114
flea markets 87
flower markets 10, 58, 96
flying times 118
Fontainebleau 93
food shops 52, 58, 59, 60
Forum des Halles 21
fountains 14, 21, 25, 32, 42,
    .... 50, 85, 92, 94, 95, 99
Foyatier, rue 84, 108
Galerie Colbert 17
Galerie Nationale de l'Image .. 16
Galerie Vivienne 17
gardens10, 14, 18, 36, 37, 40, 48,
    63, 66, 91, 92, 93, 94, 101, 106
gay 23, 114
Giverny 92
Grand Palais 55, 107
Grande Arche de La Défense . 91
grocery store 52

Halle St-Pierre 84
Harry Potter 26
holidays 118
home accessories 40
horseracing 114
Hôtel de Ville 23
Hôtel des Invalides 48
Hôtel Sully 30, 102
hotels 16, 119
Ile de la Cité 8, 96
Ile St-Louis 13, 97
Institut de France 39
Institut Français d'Architect. .. 40
insurance 118
Invalides 48
islands 8, 13, 95
Jardin d'Acclimatation 66
Jardin des Plantes 36
Jardin des Tuileries 14
Jardin du Luxembourg ... 40, 101
Jardin du Souvenir 89
Jardin Tino Rossi 36
jazz 22, 71
jewelry 16
Jewish 13, 24, 29, 31.85, 97, 104, 110
July Column 72, 103
kitchenware shop 22
language 120, 123
Latin Quarter 32
Left Bank 9, 99
Liberty Flame 61, 106
libraries 25, 75
Lido, Le 54
London 70
Louvre 18-20
Luxembourg Gardens and Palace 40, 101
Manufacture des Gobelins 76
maps 8, 11, 15, 33, 46, 47, 78, 83
Marais 23-32, 102-105
marathon 114
markets 103, 111
mealtimes 120
Memorial to the Unknown Jewish Martyr 29
Métro (Subway) 120
Métro Concorde 56, 108
money 120
Montmartre 82-87, 108-111
Montmartretrain 87

Montparnasse 77-81
Montparnasse Tower 79
mosque (Mosquée de Paris) ... 35
Moulin de la Galette 86, 110
Moulin Rouge 86, 111
museums
   American Art Museum 92
   Anatomy Museum 43
   Army Museum 48
   Centre Georges Pompidou 24, 25, 105
   Counterfeit Museum 65
   Doll Museum 26
   Edith Piaf Museum 72
   Espace Salvador-Dali 84, 109
   Fondation Cartier 77
   Fondation Mona Bismarck 62
   Galerie Nationale du Jeu de Paume 16
   Grévin Wax Museum 68
   Hunting Museum 28
   Institute for Research and Coordination of Acoustics/ Music 25
   Maison Baccarat 64
   Maison de Balzac 64
   Maison de la Culture du Japon 81
   Mitsukoshi Étoile 53
   Musée Adam Mickiewicz . 13
   Musée Adzak 79
   Musée Bourdelle 79
   Musée Carnavalet 29, 104
   Musée Cernuschi 58
   Musée Cognacq-Jay . 29, 104
   Musée d' Art Max Fourny 84
   Musée d'Art Juif 85, 110
   Musée d'Art Moderne de la Ville de Paris/Musée des Enfants 63
   Musée d'Ennery 65
   Musée d'Orsay 51
   Musée Dapper 65
   Musée de Cluny 37, 101
   Musée de l'Histoire de France/ Archives Nationales 27, 104
   Musée de l'Homme 63
   Musée de l'Orangerie des Tuileries 14
   Musée de l'Ordre de la Liberation 49

Musée de la Conciergerie 9, 96
Musée de la Marine 63
Musée de la Mode et du Textile 21
Musée de la Monnaie 39
Musée de la Musique 88
Musée de la Parfumerie 67
Musée de la Serrure/Musée Bricard 28
Musée de la Vie Romantique..69
Musée Delacroix 44
Musée des Arts Décoratifs 20
Musée des Arts et Métiers 27
Musée du Barreau de Paris 23
Musée du Luxembourg .. 101
Musée du Patrimoine et l'Architecture 63
Musée du Vieux Montmartre ... 85, 109
Musée Galliera 64
Musée Gustave-Moreau ... 69
Musée Henner 82
Musée Jacquemart-André . 60
Musée Lenine 77
Musée Librairie du Compagnonnage 42
Musée Maillol 49, 99
Musée Marmottan - Claude Monet 64
Musée National des Arts Asiatiques (Guimet) ... 63
Musée National du Louvre 18
Musée National du Sport . 65
Musée Nissim de Camondo57
Musée Pasteur 79
Musée Picasso 28, 104
Musée Zadkine 42
Museum of Advertising (Musée de la Publicité) 20
Museum of Curiosity and Magic 31
Museum of Erotic Art 87
Museum of Jewish Art and History...................... 24
Museum of Medical History39
Museum of Public Assistance35
National Museum of Modern Art 25
National Museum of Natural History...................... 36

Pinacothèque de Paris 71
Police Museum 35
Postal Museum (Musée de la Poste) 79
Rodin Museum 49
Smoking Museum 74
Tenniseum Roland-Garros 65
Veterinary Museum 90
Victor Hugo's Home 31, 102
Wine Museum 64
museum pass 9
music 88, 103, 114
Napoleon's Tomb 48
New Year's Eve 115
Notre-Dame 10, 12, 96
Obelisk of Luxor 107
opera 67, 72, 103
packing 121
Palais Abbatial 100
Palais de Chaillot 62, 63, 106
Palais de Justice.................. 9, 96
Palais de l' Élysée 55
Palais de Tokyo 63, 106
Palais Royal 17
Panthéon 37
Parc des Buttes Chaumont 88
Parc des Princes stadium 65
Parc de St-Cloud 66
Parc Floral 75
Parc Monceau 57
Parc Zoologique 75
Paris Plage. 114
Paris-Story 67
parks 57, 66, 75, 88
passages 17, 23, 71, 112
passports 121
Pavillon Elysée 54, 107
perfume 54, 67, 107
Petit Palais 55, 107
photography .. 16, 30, 60, 77, 78
Piaf, Edith 72
place de l'Alma 61, 106
place de la Bastille 72, 103
place de la Concorde 56, 107
place de la Madeleine 58
place de la Sorbonne 37, 101
place des Abbesses 82, 108
place des Pyramides 16
places des Victoires 17
place des Vosges 31, 102

place du Châtelet 95
place du Parvis Notre-Dame10, 96
place du Tertre 109
place Fürstenberg 44, 100
place Louis-Lépine 10, 96
place Pigalle 86, 111
place St-Michel 32
place Vendôme 16
Point Zéro 10
Pompidou Centre 24, 25, 105
Pont de l'Alma 61, 106
Pont Neuf........................ 8, 115
Pont St-Louis 13, 115
Pont Sully 98, 116
Pont-au-Change 95
Princess Diana 61, 62, 106
pubs 26, 61
Quartier des Horloges 25
Rambouillet 93
restaurants (by arrondissements):
   1st 17, 19
   2nd 18
   3rd 26, 27
   4th 25, 29, 30, 31, 32,
         102, 103, 104, 105
   5th 35, 37, 38
   6th 40, 41, 42, 43, 100, 101
   7th 48, 49, 51, 52, 99
   8th 56
   9th 67, 68, 69
   10th 71
   11th 73
   12th 74
   13th 75, 76
   14th 77, 80
   15th 80
   16th 64
   18th 84, 86, 109, 110
   19th 88
   20th 90
rest rooms 58, 121
Rivoli, rue de 20
Rodin Museum 49
Roland-Garros Stadium 65
Roman arena 36
Sacred Heart Basilica
   (Sacré-Coeur) 82, 108

safety 121
Samaritaine, La 95
sculpture garden (outdoor) 36
Sewers (Les Egouts) 52
shoe, shopping 27, 50
shopping mall 20, 21, 121
smoking 74, 120
Sorbonne, La 37, 101
Square de l'Ile de France 97
Square du Vert-Galant 13
Square Jean XIII 97
Square René-Viviani 34
Square Suzanne Buisson 110
stamp market 55
Stravinsky Fountain 25
synagogue 69
taxes (Value Added Tax) 122
tea shops 56, 57, 60
telephone 122
tennis 65, 114
time 122
tipping 117, 122
Tour de France 114
train stations 70, 74
Trocadéro Gardens 63, 106
Trompe l'Oeil Mural 60
UNESCO Headquarters 45
Val-de-Grâce 38
Vaux-le-Vicomte 93
Versailles 91
Village St-Paul 30, 102
vineyard 85, 109
walks ....
   Islands 95-99
   Left Bank 99-102
   Marais 102-105
   Major Sights 105-108
   Montmartre 108-111
   Culinary 111-112
water 122
water park 81
weather 122
web sites 122
windmill 86, 110
wine bars 17, 21, 59, 110
wine shops 17, 57, 59, 100
zoos 36, 66, 75

OPEN ROAD PUBLISHING

Look for all of Open Road's *new* European travel and menu-reader guides:

- Paris Made Easy, $9.95
- London Made Easy, $9.95
- Rome Made Easy, $9.95 (Spring 2005)
- Provence Made Easy, $9.95 (Spring 2005)
- Eating & Drinking in Paris, $9.95
- Eating & Drinking in Italy, $9.95
- Eating & Drinking in Spain, $9.95

For US orders, include $4.00 for postage and handling for the first book ordered; for each additional book, add $1.00. Orders outside US, inquire first about shipping charges (money order payable in US dollars on US banks only for overseas shipments). Send to:

Open Road Publishing
PO Box 284, Cold Spring Harbor, NY 11724

NEW EUROPEAN GUIDES